SPOKEN
FRENCH

anglais français
tent - tante
campers

SECOND EDITION

SPOKEN FRENCH
for students and travelers

Bernard F. Uzan
Middlebury College
Graduate Summer School

Charles E. Kany
Mathurin Dondo

D. C. HEATH AND COMPANY
Lexington, Massachusetts   Toronto

Published simultaneously in Canada.

Printed in the United States of America.

International Standard Book Number: 0-669-00878-8

Library of Congress Catalog Card Number: 77-75021

PREFACE

Much time has gone by since the first edition of *Spoken French for Students and Travelers,* but it has nevertheless shown a remarkable staying power. Because of this, it was felt that an updated edition should be published.

The purpose of this book is to offer easy but adequate conversational French to students of the language (in colleges and high schools, and in adult education courses) and to travelers in general. The book may be considered a basic conversational text not only for beginners who have no knowledge of French, but also for those who already possess a foundation. A skeleton grammar is appended for the benefit of those who may wish to consult it. To this end, footnoted references will be found throughout the text corresponding to explanatory paragraphs in the Appendix.

In preparing this new edition, I have largely replaced the original dialogues with situations in dialogue form that deal with how to meet people, how to reach Paris from the airport, how to get around by bicycle, how to use the French telephone system, and so forth. The English translation given for each French phrase is a time-saving device particularly helpful for self-instruction, as is also the phonetic transcription that now appears throughout the book.

New sections, *Remarques,* explain French customs when the situations lend themselves to this treatment. Part 6, especially, contains practical information on places to stay or ways to travel.

If composition is required, students may prepare situations similar to those in the book. Furthermore, the teacher may formulate his or her own questions in French concerning the material under study.

Bernard F. Uzan

CONTENTS

4   Les achats et les services

5   Divertissements et excursions

6   Pour les jeunes

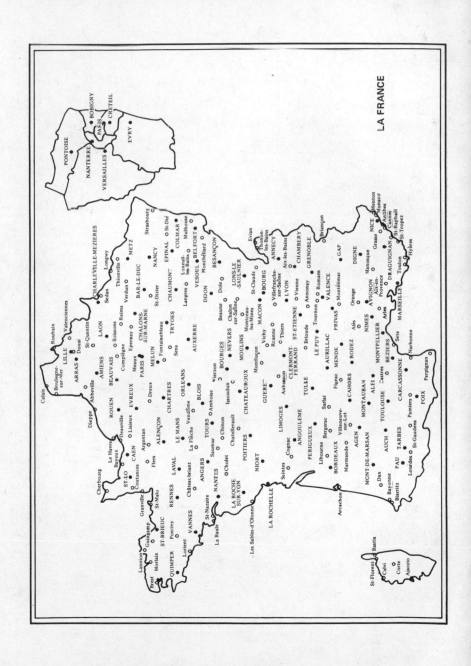

LA FRANCE

PRONUNCIATION

The *approximate* English equivalents of the phonetic symbols are as follows:

[i]	pol*i*ce		[u]	b*oo*t
[e]	g*a*te		[k]	*c*at
[ɛ]	m*e*t		[g]	*g*o
[a]	p*a*t		[s]	*s*o
[ɑ]	f*a*ther		[z]	*z*ero
[ɔ]	cl*o*th		[ʃ]	*sh*e
[o]	v*o*te		[ʒ]	a*z*ure

[ɲ] only approximately like o*ni*on, with greater contact area of tongue and palate and less *i*.

[y] no equivalent. Round lips as for [u] and try to pronounce [i].

[ø] no equivalent. Round lips as for [o] and try to pronounce [e].

[œ] no equivalent. Round lips as for [ɔ] and try to pronounce [ɛ].

[r] may be uvular or lingual. In the lingual *r* the tip of tongue vibrates against hard palate. In the uvular *r* (standard

1

among cultivated French) the uvula vibrates against the back of the tongue.

[ə]   as in sof*a*, but with lips rounded.

[ɛ̃]
[ɑ̃]   In these nasalized vowels, allow breath to pass through
[ɔ̃]   mouth and nasal passages at same time.
[œ̃]

[j]   as in *y*es.

[ɥ]   like [y] pronounced rapidly.

The following symbols are pronounced approximately as in English: [w], [p], [t], [d], [f], [v], [m], [n], [l].

Sounds enclosed in parentheses are generally pronounced in slow, careful speech and omitted in rapid, familiar speech: **Je vais aller en France** /ʒ(ə) vɛ(z) ale ɑ̃ frɑ̃ːs/ *I am going to France*.

No attempt has been made to group the phonetic symbols. Closely related words should be read as a unit.

The symbol [ː] is used to indicate length.

Expressions courantes

Useful Expressions

Un Américain à Paris

An American in Paris

■ **Quelques expressions pour tous les jours**   *Some everyday expressions*

oui /wi/ *yes*
non /nɔ̃/ *no*
s'il vous plaît /si(l) vu plɛ/ *please*
merci /mɛrsi/ *thank you*
merci beaucoup /mɛrsi boku/ *thank you very much*
⌣ il n'y a pas de quoi /i(l) n ja pɑ d kwa/ *you're welcome*
de rien /də rjɛ̃/ *you're welcome*

■ **Salutations** *Greetings*

Bonjour /bɔ̃ʒuːr/ *Good morning/good afternoon*
Bonne nuit /bɔn nɥi/ *Good night*
Bonsoir /bɔ̃swaːr/ *Good evening*
Au revoir /ɔ rəvwaːr/ *Good-bye*
A bientôt /a bjɛ̃to/ *See you later*

■ **Parlez-vous français?** *Do you speak French?*

Je comprends. . . /ʒə kɔ̃prɑ̃/ *I understand . . .*
Je ne comprends pas. . . /ʒə n(ə) kɔ̃prɑ̃ pɑ/ *I don't understand . . .*
Parlez plus lentement. /parle ply lɑ̃tmɑ̃/ *Speak more slowly.*
Je suis Américain. /ʒə sɥiz‿amerikɛ̃/ *I am an American.*
Je parle un peu français. /ʒə parl œ̃ pø frɑ̃sɛ/ *I speak a little French.*

Pouvez-vous me dire... /puve vu mə diːr/ *Could you tell me* . . .

Pouvez-vous m'aider... /puve vu mɛde/ *Could you help me* . . .

Puis-je avoir... /pɥiʒ avwaːr/ *May I have* . . .

Pouvez-vous m'indiquer... /puve vu mẽdike/ *Can you show me* . . .

■ **Problèmes** *Problems*

Je suis perdu. /ʒə sɥi pɛrdy/ *I am lost.*

J'ai perdu ma valise. /ʒe pɛrdy ma valiz/ *I have lost my suitcase.*

Je suis fatigué. /ʒə sɥi fatige/ *I am tired.*

J'ai peur. /ʒe pœr/ *I am afraid.*

J'ai faim. ʒe fɛ̃/ *I am hungry.*

J'ai soif. /ʒe swaf/ *I am thirsty.*

Je suis malade. /ʒə sɥi ᴍalad/ *I am sick.*

Où est la sortie? /u ɛ la sɔrti/ *Where is the exit?*

Où sont les taxis? /u sɔ̃ le taksi/ *Where are the taxis?*

Où suis-je? /u sɥiʒ/ *Where am I?*

Où est-ce? /u ɛs/ *Where is it?*

■ **Présentations** *Introductions*

Je vous présente Monsieur/ Madame/ Mademoiselle . . . (formal)
/ʒə vu prezɑ̃t məsjø madam madəmwazɛl/
This is Mr./Mrs./Miss . . .

Enchanté de faire votre connaissance.
/ɑ̃ʃɑ̃te d(ə) fɛr vɔt(r) kɔnɛsɑ̃ːs/
Nice to meet you.

Monsieur Dupont, Madame Smith. (informal)
/məsjø dypɔ̃ madam Smit/
Mr. Dupont, Mrs. Smith.

■ Les jours　*Days*

lundi　/lœ̃di/　Monday
mardi　/mardi/　Tuesday
mercredi　/mɛrkrədi/　Wednesday
jeudi　/ʒødi/　Thursday
vendredi　/vɑ̃drədi/　Friday
samedi　/samdi/　Saturday
dimanche　/dimɑ̃ːʃ/　Sunday

le matin　/lə matɛ̃/　the morning
la journée　/la ʒurne/　the work day
l'après-midi　/laprɛ midi/　the afternoon
le soir　/lə swaːr/　the evening
la nuit　/la nɥi/　the night
une semaine　/yn səmɛn/　a week
la semaine dernière　/la smɛn dɛrnjɛr/　last week
le mois prochain　/lə mwɑ prɔʃɛ̃/　next month
le weekend (fin de semaine)　/lə wikɛnd (fɛ̃ də smɛn)/　the weekend
les vacances　/le vakɑ̃ːs/　vacation

Quel jour sommes-nous?　/kɛl ʒuːr sɔm nu/　What day is it?
Aujourd'hui, c'est lundi.　/oʒurdɥi sɛ lœ̃di/　Today is Monday.
demain　/dəmɛ̃/　tomorrow
après demain　/aprɛ dmɛ̃/　the day after tomorrow
hier　/jɛːr/　yesterday
avant-hier　/avɑ̃tjɛːr/　the day before yesterday
la veille　/la vɛːj/　the eve, day before

■ Les nombres   *Numbers*

```
 1 un, une   /œ̃ yn/
 2 deux   /dø/
 3 trois   /trwɑ/
 4 quatre   /katr/
 5 cinq   /sɛ̃:k/
 6 six   /sis/
 7 sept   /sɛt/
 8 huit   /ɥit/
 9 neuf   /nœf/
10 dix   /dis/
11 onze   /ɔ̃:z/
12 douze   /du:z/
13 treize   /trɛ:z/
14 quatorze   /katɔrz/
15 quinze   /kɛ̃:z/
16 seize   /sɛ:z/
17 dix-sept   /di sɛt/
18 dix-huit   /diz‿ɥit/
19 dix-neuf   /diz nœf/
20 vingt   /vɛ̃/
21 vingt et un(e)   /vɛ̃te œ̃ (yn)/
22 vingt-deux   /vɛ̃ dø/
23 vingt-trois, etc.   /vɛ̃ trwa/
30 trente   /trɑ̃:t/
31 trente et un(e)   /trɑ̃t‿e œ̃ (yn)/
32 trente-deux, etc.   /trɑ̃t dø/
40 quarante   /karɑ̃:t/
41 quarante et un(e)   /karɑ̃t‿e œ̃ (yn)/
42 quarante-deux, etc.   /karɑ̃t dø/
50 cinquante   /sɛ̃kɑ̃:t/
51 cinquante et un(e)   /sɛ̃kɑ̃t‿e œ̃ (yn)/
52 cinquante-deux, etc.   /sɛ̃kɑ̃t dø/
60 soixante   /swasɑ̃:t/
```

61 **soixante et un(e)** /swasãt‿e œ̃ (yn)/
62 **soixante-deux, etc.** /swasãt dø/
70 **soixante-dix** /swasãt dis/
71 **soixante et onze** /swasãt‿e ɔ̃ːz/
72 **soixante-douze** /swasãt duːz/
73 **soixante-treize** /swasãtrɛːz/
74 **soixante-quatorze** /swasãt katɔrz/
75 **soixante-quinze** /swasãt kɛ̃ːz/
76 **soixante-seize** /swasãt sɛːz/
77 **soixante-dix-sept** /swasãt di sɛt/
78 **soixante-dix-huit** /swasãt diz‿ɥit/
79 **soixante-dix-neuf** /swasãt diz nœf/
80 **quatre-vingts** /katrə vɛ̃/
81 **quatre-vingt-un(e)** /katrə vɛ̃ œ̃ (yn)/
82 **quatre-vingt-deux, etc.** /katrə vɛ̃ dø/
90 **quatre-vingt-dix** /katrə vɛ̃ dis/
91 **quatre-vingt-onze** /katrə vɛ̃ ɔ̃ːz/
92 **quatre-vingt-douze** /katrə vɛ̃ duːz/
93 **quatre-vingt-treize** /katrə vɛ̃ trɛːz/
94 **quatre-vingt-quatorze** /katrə vɛ̃ katɔrz/
95 **quatre-vingt-quinze** /katrə vɛ̃ kɛ̃ːz/
96 **quatre-vingt-seize** /katrə vɛ̃ sɛːz/
97 **quatre-vingt-dix-sept** /katrə vɛ̃ di sɛt/
98 **quatre-vingt-dix-huit** /katrə vɛ̃ diz‿ɥit/
99 **quatre-vingt-dix-neuf** /katrə vɛ̃ diz nœf/
100 **cent** /sã/
101 **cent un** /sã œ̃/
102 **cent deux, etc.** /sã dø/
200 **deux cents** /dø sã/
1000 **mille** /mil/
1001 **mille un** /mil œ̃/
1002 **mille deux, etc.** /mil dø/
1500 **mille cinq cents** or **quinze cents** /mil sɛ̃ sã/ or /kɛ̃z sã/
2000 **deux mille** /dø mil/
1,000,000 **un million** /œ̃ miljɔ̃/

■ **Poids et mesures**   *Weights and measures*

16 (20) onces (oz.) = 1 pinte (pt.)	2 pintes (pt.) = 1 quart (qt.)
100 g = 3,5 oz.	½ kg = 1,1 livre (lb.)
200 g = 7,0 oz.	1 kg = 2, 2lb.
1 oz. = 28,35 g	1 lb. = 453,60 g

4 quarts (qt.) = 1 gallon (gal.)	1 quart = 0,95 (1,14) 1
1 litre (l) = 1,06 (0,88) quarts	1 gallon = 3,8 (4,5) 1

The numbers in parentheses represent the Canadian standard.

■ **Milles en kilomètres**   *Miles to kilometers*

1 mille = 1,609 km

milles	10	20	30	40	50	60	70	80	90	100
km.	16	32	48	64	80	97	113	129	145	161

■ **Mesures de capacité**   *Liquid measures*

litres	gallons américains	gallons canadiens	litres	gallons américains	gallons canadiens
5	1.3	1.1	30	7.8	6.6
10	2.6	2.2	35	9.1	7.7
15	3.9	3.3	40	10.4	8.8
20	5.2	4.4	45	11.7	9.9
25	6.5	5.5	50	13.0	11.0

■ **Kilomètres en milles**   *Kilometers to miles*

1 km = 0,62 mille

km.	10	20	30	40	50	60	70	80	90	100	110	120	130
milles	6	12	19	25	31	37	44	50	56	62	68	75	81

■ **Poids**   *Weight*

The number in the center represents both kilos and pounds.
For example, 1 kilo = 2.20 lbs. and 1 lb. = 0.45 kilos.

Kilogrammes		Livres
0,45	**1**	2,205
0,90	**2**	4,405
1,35	**3**	6,614
1,80	**4**	8,818
2,25	**5**	11,023
2,70	**6**	13,227
3,15	**7**	15,432
3,60	**8**	17,636
4,05	**9**	19,840
4,50	**10**	22,045
6,75	**15**	33,068
9,00	**20**	44,889
11,25	**25**	55,113
22,50	**50**	110,225
33,75	**75**	165,338
45,00	**100**	220,450

■ Mètres et pieds   *Meters and feet*

The number in the center represents both meters and feet. For example, 1 meter = 3.28 feet and 1 foot = 0.30 meter.

Mètres		Pieds
0,30	**1**	3,281
0,61	**2**	6,563
0,91	**3**	9,843
1,22	**4**	13,124
1,52	**5**	16,403
1,83	**6**	19,686
2,13	**7**	22,967
2,44	**8**	26,248
2,74	**9**	29,529
3,05	**10**	32,810
3,35	**11**	36,091
3,66	**12**	39,372
3,96	**13**	42,635
4,27	**14**	45,934
4,57	**15**	49,215
4,88	**16**	52,496
5,18	**17**	55,777
5,49	**18**	59,058
5,79	**19**	62,339
6,10	**20**	65,620
7,62	**25**	82,023
15,24	**50**	164,046
22,86	**75**	246,069
30,48	**100**	328,092

■ **Pouces et centimètres**   *Inches and centimeters*

To change centimeters into inches,
multiply by 0.39.
To change inches into centimeters,
multiply by 2.54.

Centimeters	Inches
0	0.0
1	0.5
2	1.0
3	1.5
4	
5	2.0
6	2.5
7	3.0
8	
9	3.5
10	4.0

1 cm. = 0.3937 in.
1 in. = 2.54001 cm.

■ La température   *Temperature*

To change degrees F to degrees C, subtract 32 and multiply by $\frac{5}{9}$.
$(F - 32) \times \frac{5}{9} = C.$
To change degrees C to degrees F, multiply by $\frac{9}{5}$ and add 32.
$(C \times \frac{9}{5}) + 32 = F.$

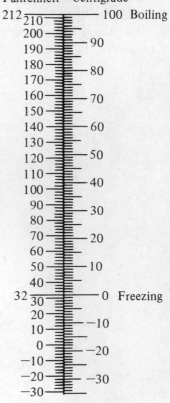

$F = 32 + \frac{9}{5}C$
$C = \frac{5}{9}(F - 32)$

■ **L'heure**   *The time*

Quelle heure est-il?   /kɛl œr ɛt‿il/   *What time is it?*
Il est   /il ɛ/   *It is:*

midi
midi

midi et quart
midi e kaːr

une heure vingt
yn œr vɛ̃

2h 25
døz‿œr vɛ̃ sɛ̃ːk

3h et demie
trwɑz‿œr e dmi

5h moins 25
sɛ̃k œr mwɛ̃ vɛ̃ sɛ̃ːk

6h moins vingt
siz‿œr mwɛ̃ vɛ̃

7h moins le quart
sɛt œr mwɛ̃ l kaːr

8h moins 10
ɥit œr mwɛ̃ dis

9h moins 5
nœv œr mwɛ̃ sɛ̃ːk

10h
diz‿œːr

11h 5
ɔ̃ːz‿œr sɛ̃ːk

Excusez-moi, vous avez l'heure si'l vous plaît?
/ɛkskyze mwa vuz‿ave   lœːr   si(l) vu   plɛ/
Excuse me, do you have the time please?

A quelle heure est la fermeture/l'ouverture du magasin?
/a kɛl   œr   ɛ   la fɛrmətyr/luvɛrtyr   dy magazɛ̃/
What time does the store close/open?

Nous pouvons vous donner rendez-vous demain à deux heures
/nu   puvɔ̃   vu   dɔne   rɑ̃de   vu   d(ə)mɛ̃ a døz‿œr
et demie.
e   dmi/
We could give you an appointment tomorrow at 2:30.

A quelle heure part/arrive l'avion?
/a kɛl   œr   paːr/ariv   lavjɔ̃/
What time does the plane leave/arrive?

Combien de temps durera le film?
/kɔ̃bjɛ̃   d tɑ̃   dyrəra l(ə) film/
How long will the movie last?

A quelle heure dois-je arriver?
/a kɛl   œr   dwaʒ arive/
What time should I arrive?

REMARQUES

When indicating the time of trains, buses, theatrical performances, radio programs and all public functions in general, the twenty-four-hour system is used: time is counted from twelve noon to twenty-four (midnight). Thus **quinze heures** (*fifteen o'clock*) = *three* P.M. This official practice, however, is not extended to ordinary conversation.

Vous allez en France?

Are You Going to France?

Bonjour, Philippe.
/bɔ̃ʒuːr   filip/
Good morning, Philip.

Ah, bonjour, René!
/a   bɔ̃ʒuːr   rəne/
Oh, good morning, René!

Qu'est-ce que vous allez faire cet été?[1]
/k   ɛ   s   kə   vuz‿ale   fɛːrsɛt‿ete/
What are you going to do this summer?

Je   vais aller en France![2]
/ʒ(ə) vɛ(z) ale   ɑ̃   frɑ̃ːs/
I'm going to France.

Vraiment? Quand partez-vous?
/vrɛmɑ̃   kɑ̃   parte vu/
Really? When do you leave?

Je   pars lundi prochain.
/ʒ(ə) paːr lœ̃di   prɔʃɛ̃/
I leave next Monday.

Pour combien de temps?
/pur kɔ̃bjɛ̃   t tɑ̃/
How long (will you be away) for?

---

[1] Interrogative forms. § 23.   [2] § 2d.

Pour trois mois environ.
/pur trwɑ mwɑ ɑ̃virɔ̃/
> For about three months.

Vous allez rester à Paris?
/vuz‿ale   rɛste a pari/
> Are you going to stay in Paris?

Deux ou trois semaines seulement.
/dø(z) u trwɑ smɛːn   sœlmɑ̃/
> Only two or three weeks.

Vous allez visiter toute l'Europe?
/vuz‿ale   vizite tut   l œrɔp/
> Are you going to visit all of Europe?

Oh, non! seulement la France.
/o, nɔ̃ sœlmɑ̃   la frɑ̃ːs/
> Oh, no! only France.

Alors, vous allez faire un beau voyage.
/alɔːr, vuz‿ale   fɛr œ̃ bo   vwajaːʒ/
> Then you're going to have a beautiful trip.

J'espère que oui.
/ʒ ɛspɛːr kə wi/
> I hope so.

REMARQUES

1. Other seasons are: **le printemps** /lə prɛ̃tɑ̃/, *spring*; **l'automne** /lotɔn/ m., *fall*; **l'hiver** /livɛːr/ m., *winter*.

2. Some other countries are: **l'Angleterre** /lɑ̃glətɛːr/ f., *England*; **l'Italie** /litali/ f.; *Italy*; **l'Allemagne** /lalmaɲ/ f., *Germany*. Cf. § 2*d*.

La lettre

The Letter

Avez-vous quelque chose pour écrire?
/ave vu kɛlkə   ʃoːz pur ekriːr/
Do you have something to write with?

Oui. Pourquoi?
/wi   purkwa/
Yes. Why?

Je veux écrire des lettres.
/ʒə vø(z) ekriːr de lɛt(r)/
I want to write some letters.

J'ai un stylo. Tenez.
/ʒ e œ̃ stilo   tǝne/
I have a pen. Here.

Merci. Vous êtes bien aimable.
/mɛrsi vuz‿ɛt   bjɛ̃‿ɛmabl/
Thank you. That's really nice of you.

Avez-vous du papier à lettres?
/ave vu   dy papje a lɛt(r)/
Do you have (some) writing paper?

Oui, j'ai du papier et des enveloppes.
/wi   ʒ ə dy papje e dez‿ɑ̃vlɔp/
Yes, I've got paper and envelopes.

Avez-vous des timbres aussi?
/ave vu   de tɛ̃ːbr   osi/
  Do you have stamps, too?

Ah, non, je n'ai pas de timbres.
/ɑ   nɔ̃   ʒ   n e   pɑ   t   tɛ̃ːbr/
  Oh, no, I don't have any stamps.

Quels timbres voulez-vous?
/kɛl   tɛ̃ːbr   vule   vu/
  What (kind of) stamps do you want?

Deux à soixante centimes.
/dø   a swasɑ̃t   sɑ̃tim/
  Two sixty-centime stamps.

Tenez. Voilà.
/təne   vwala/
  Here. There you are.

Merci.
/mɛrsi/
  Thank you.

Il   n'y a pas de quoi.
/i(l) n j   a   pɑ   t   kwa/
  You're welcome.

La famille

The Family

Vous avez écrit[1] à votre famille?
/vuz‿ave(z)ekri   a vɔt(r) famiːj/
> *Have you written to your family?*

Oui, j'ai écrit deux lettres.
/wi   ʒ e ekri dø   lɛt(r)/
> *Yes, I've written two letters.*

A qui avez-vous écrit?
/a ki   ave vu(z) ekri/
> *Who have you written to?*

A mon père, à ma mère et à Paul.[2]
/a mɔ̃   pɛːr a ma mɛːr e a pɔl/
> *To my father, my mother, and Paul.*

Vous écrivez beaucoup de lettres?
/vuz‿ekrive   boku   d(ə) lɛt(r)/
> *Do you write many letters?*

J'écris souvent à mes parents.
/ʒ ekri suvɑ̃   a me   parɑ̃/
> *I write frequently to my parents (or relatives).*

Où est votre ami Paul à présent?
/u ɛ vɔtr ami pɔl a prezɑ̃/
> *Where's your friend Paul now?*

[1] Perfect tense. §33, II. [2] Possessive adjectives, §9.

Il est à New York.
/il ɛ(t) a/
> *He's in New York.*

Son frère est à New York aussi?
/sɔ̃ frɛːr ɛ(t) a   osi/
> *Is his brother in New York, too?*

Non, il est en France maintenant.
/nɔ̃ il ɛ(t) ã frãs   mɛ̃tnã/
> *No, he's in France now.*

Qu'est-ce que Paul fait à New York?
/k ɛ s kə pɔl fɛ a/
> *What's Paul doing in New York?*

Il étudie la médecine.
/il etydi la medsin/
> *He's studying medicine.*

C'est une profession bien dangereuse.
/sɛt yn prɔfɛsjɔ̃ bjɛ̃ dãʒrøːz/
> *That's a dangerous profession.*

Pas pour Paul, mais pour ses clients.
/pɑ pur pɔl mɛ pur se kliã/
> *Not for Paul, but for his patients (lit. " clients ").*

REMARQUES

1. Other relatives: **la sœur** /sœːr/, *sister*; **l'oncle** /lɔ̃ːkl/ m., *uncle*; **la tante** /tãːt/, *aunt*; **le cousin** /kuzɛ̃/, (*male*) *cousin*; **la cousine** /kuzin/, (*female*) *cousin*.

2. Paul could also be studying **le droit** /drwa/, *law*, or **les langues** /le lãːg/ f., *languages*.

Seul(e) en France

Alone in France

Comment allez-vous?
/kɔmɑ̃t ale vu/
   How are you?

Permettez-moi de me présenter, Richard... /Nicole...
/pɛrmɛte mwa d mə prezɑ̃te riʃaːr nikɔl/
   Let me introduce myself, Richard . . . /Nicole . . .

Depuis combien de temps êtes-vous ici?
/dəpɥi kɔ̃bjɛ̃ d tɑ̃ ɛt vu ʲisi/
   How long have you been here?

Vous êtes ici de temps depuis combien ?

Vous venez souvent ici?
/vu vne suvɑ̃ isi/ → *often*
   Do you come here often? *rarement*

Est-ce que vous vous plaisez ici?
/ɛ s kə vu vu plɛze isi/
   Do you like it here?

Quelle belle journée!
/kɛl bɛl ʒurne/
   What a beautiful day!

Il fait un temps horrible.
/i(l) fɛ(t) œ̃ tɑ̃ ɔribl/
   It is terrible weather.

D'où venez-vous?
/du vne vu/
  Where are you from?

feu really means fire.

Avez-vous du feu?
/ave vu   dy fø/
  Do you have a light?

lumière
les
~~tests~~ Etats Unis
d'amérique

glass

Voulez-vous prendre un verre avec moi?
/vule vu prã:dr œ̃ vɛr avɛk mwa/
  Would you like to have a drink with me?

Attendez-vous quelqu'un?
/atãde   vu   kɛlkœ̃/
  Are you waiting for someone?

sans - without
souci - care

Voulez-vous sortir avec moi ce soir?
/vule   vu   sɔrtir avɛk mwa sə swa:r/
  Would you like to go out with me tonight?

Voulez-vous dîner avec moi?
/vule   vu   dine avɛk mwa/
  Would you like to have dinner with me?

J'aimerais vous inviter au cinéma/au théâtre.
/ʒɛmrɛ   vuz‿ɛ̃vite   o sinema/o teatr/
  I'd like to invite you to the movies/to the theater.

Aimez-vous danser?
/ɛme   vu   dãse/
  Do you like to dance?

Etes-vous libre ce soir?
/ɛt   vu   libr sə swa:r/
  Are you free this evening?

Voyagez-vous seul(e)?
/vwajaʒe vu   sœl/
> *Are you traveling alone?*

Où logez-vous?
/u   lɔʒe   vu/
> *Where are you staying?*

Quel est votre numéro de téléphone?
/kɛl ɛ vɔtr nymero d telefɔn/
> *What is your phone number?*

Puis-je vous ramener chez vous?
/pɥi ʒ vu   ramne   ʃe   vu/
> *May I take you home?*

Le temps

The Weather

Quel temps fait-il aujourd'hui?
/kɛl tã   fɛt_il oʒurdɥi/
How's the weather?

Il   fait beau /mauvais/frais/humide/doux/bon.
/i(l) fɛ bo   mɔvɛ   frɛ   ymid   du   bɔ̃/
   It's fine/bad/cool/humid/mild/warm (weather).

Aimez-vous la chaleur?
/ɛme   vu   la ʃalœːr/
   Do you like the heat?

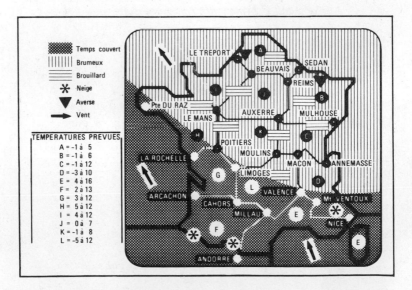

Oui, mais je   n'aime pas le froid.
/wi   mɛ   ʒ(ə) n ɛm   pɑ l frwa/
> Yes, but I don't like the cold.

Moi   non plus.
/mwa nɔ̃   ply/
> Neither do I (lit. " I no more ").

Vous êtes comme moi.
/vuz‿ɛt   kɔm   mwa/
> You're like me.

■ **Les mois et les saisons**   *The months and the seasons*

Fait-il froid en hiver?
/fɛt‿il frwa ɑ̃n‿ivɛːr/
> Is it cold in winter?

Janvier et février sont pluvieux et assez froids.
/ʒɑ̃vje   e fevrije sɔ̃   plyvjø   e ase   frwa/
> January and February are rainy and somewhat cold.

Allez-vous en vacances en été?
/ale   vuz‿ɑ̃   vakɑ̃s   ɑ̃n‿ete/
> Do you go on vacation in summer?

En juillet, je   reste à Paris; en août je   vais à la plage.
/ɑ̃ ʒɥijɛ   ʒ(ə) rɛst a pari   ɑ̃n‿u   ʒ(ə) vɛz‿a la plaʒ/
> In July I stay in Paris; in August I go to the beach.

Et en automne?
/e ɑ̃n‿otɔn/
> And in the fall?

Septembre est le mois de la rentrée des classes.
/sɛptɑ̃ːbr   ɛ lə mwɑ d la rɑ̃tre   de klɑs/
> September is the month when classes begin.

Le printemps, est-elle la saison la plus agréable?
/lə prɛ̃tɑ̃   ɛt‿ɛl   la sɛzɔ̃   la plyz‿agreabl/
Is spring the most pleasant season?

REMARQUES

Other expressions for the weather: **il fait clair de lune** /klɛr də lyn/, *there is moonlight*; **glissant** /glisɑ̃/, *slippery*; **il fait du vent** or **il y a du vent**/ dy vɑ̃/, *it is windy*; **il neige**/ i nɛ:ʒ/, *it is snowing*; **il gèle** /i ʒɛ:l/, *it is freezing*; **la tempête** /tɑ̃pɛ:t/, *storm*; **le brouillard** /bruja:r/, *fog*.

2

L'arrivée

Arriving

A l'aéroport

At the Airport

REMARQUES

You are now in France, and you have to speak or at least understand the language. Your plane arrived in Paris at the new airport Roissy-Charles de Gaulle. Your first contact with France is not the most agreeable—customs and police; the remainder of your trip should be more pleasant.

Americans do not need a visa; a passport is sufficient.

■ **Contrôle de police**   *Police*

Monsieur, votre passeport s'il vous plaît.
/məsjø   vɔt(r) paspɔr   si(l) vu   plɛ/
   Sir, your passport please.

Le voici.
/lə vwasi/
   Here it is.

Combien de temps resterez-vous?
/kɔ̃bjɛ̃   d tɑ̃   rɛstəre vu/
   How long will you be staying?

Je resterai quelques jours/une semaine/un mois.
/ʒə rɛstəre kɛlkə   ʒuːr   yn   səmɛn   œ̃ mwa/
   I'll be staying a few days/a week/a month.

Vous êtes en voyage d'affaires?
/vuz‿ɛt   ɑ̃ vwajaʒ dafɛːr/
You're on a business trip?

Non, je suis ici en vacances.
/nɔ̃   ʒə sɥiz‿isi ɑ̃ vakɑ̃ːs/
No, I'm here on vacation.

Et vous madame, avez-vous votre carte de débarquement?
/e vu   madam   ave   vu   vɔt(r) kart də debarkmɑ̃/
And you ma'am, do you have your disembarkation card?

Je suis en transit.
/ʒə sɥiz‿ɑ̃ trɑ̃zit/
I am in transit.

■ **Douanes**   *Customs*

Monsieur, avez-vous quelque chose à déclarer?
/məsjø   ave vu   kɛlkə   ʃoz   a deklare/
Sir, do you have anything to declare?

Non, seulement quelques souvenirs pour la famille/pour des
/nɔ̃   sœlmɑ̃   kɛlkə   suvnir   pur la famiːj pur dez‿
amis.
ami/
No, only some souvenirs for my family/for friends.

Veuillez ouvrir cette valise.
/vœje   uvriːr sɛt   valiz/
Would you mind opening this suitcase.

J'ai une cartouche de cigarettes et une bouteille d'alcool.
/ʒe yn kartuʃ   də sigarɛt   e yn butɛːj   dalkɔl
Dois-je payer pour cela?
dwa ʒ pɛje pur sla/
*I have a carton of cigarettes and a bottle of liquor. Do I
have to pay for that?*

Non. Avez-vous d'autres bagages?
/nɔ̃   ave   vu   doːtrə   bagaʒ/
> *No. Do you have any other suitcases?*

Oui, une autre valise, mais je n'ai que des objets personnels.
/wi   yn   oːtrə   valiz   mɛ   ʒ(ə) ne kə   dez‿ɔbʒɛ   pɛrsɔnɛl/
> *Yes, one other suitcase, but I only have personal articles.*

Bon, ça va; vous pouvez passer. Vous n'avez pas de droits de
/bɔ̃   sa va   vu   puve   pɑse   vu   nave   pɑ   d   drwa   də

douane à payer.
dwan   a pɛje/
> *Fine, that will do; you can go ahead. You don't have to pay duty.*

■ **Les bagages—Le porteur**   *Luggage—The porter*

REMARQUES

Usually you will find a push-cart on the platform to help you move your luggage yourself. However, there are not always enough carts and you may have to call a porter.

Porteur, prenez ces valises s'il vous plaît.
/pɔrtœːr   prəne   se   valiz   si(l) vu   plɛ/
> *Porter, would you take these suitcases.*

Lesquelles, monsieur?
/lekɛl   məsjø/
> *Which ones, sir?*

Les deux grandes, la bleue et la noire.
/le   dø   grɑ̃d   la blø   e la nwaːr/
> *The two big ones, the blue one and the black one.*

Bien monsieur! Vous prenez le bus ou un taxi?
/bjɛ̃ məsjø   vu   prəne l(ə) bys u ɶ̃ taksi/
    O.K. sir! Are you taking the bus or a taxi?

Un taxi. Ah! J'ai aussi un petit sac écossais.
/ɶ̃ taksi ɑ   ʒe osi ɶ̃ pti sak ekɔsɛ/
    A taxi. Oh! I've got a small plaid bag, too.

Voilà monsieur.
/vwala məsjø/
    Here you are sir.

Combien vous dois-je?
/kɔ̃bjɛ̃   vu   dwa ʒ/
    What do I owe you?

■ **Le change**   *Currency exchange*

> REMARQUES
>
> You will find an exchange counter in most international airports where you can change your dollars or traveler's checks. Certain traveler's checks will be refused in many establishments in France.
>
> You must have a minimal amount of francs for the bus (where foreign currency is not accepted) or the taxi (where foreign currency, if accepted, is taken at a lower rate of exchange).

Je voudrais changer des dollars en argent français.
/ʒə vudrɛ   ʃɑ̃ʒe   de dɔlar ɑ̃n‿arʒɑ̃ frɑ̃sɛ/
    I'd like to change dollars into French currency.

Oui monsieur. Combien?
/wi məsjø   kɔ̃bjɛ̃/
    Yes sir. How much?

Quel est le taux de change?
/kɛl ɛ   l(ə)to d ʃɑ̃ːʒ/
    What is the rate of exchange?

Le taux est de...
/lə to   ɛ də/
    The rate is . . .

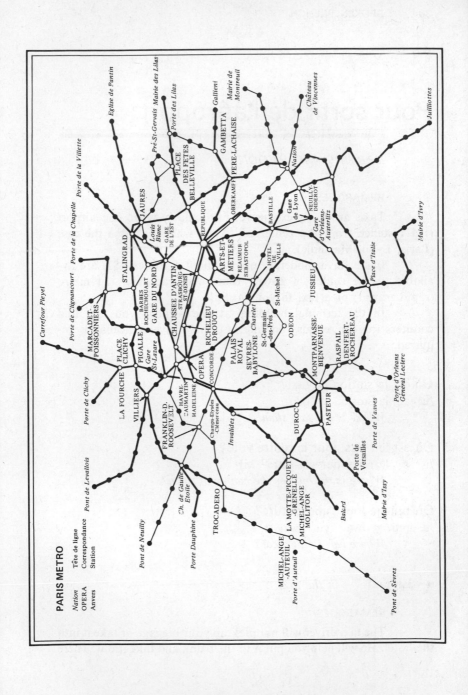

PARIS METRO

Nation   Tête de ligne
OPERA   Correspondance
Anvers   Station

Pour sortir de l'aéroport

Leaving the Airport

REMARQUES

Taxis are fairly expensive, particularly when the airport is a distance from the center of town, which is often the case (Paris, Lyon, Marseille).

Buses for a moderate price (about 5 francs—$1) are available to the center of town; there you can take the métro (rapid transit) or a taxi to your hotel.

In the terminal building at the airport you can find counters for car rentals; an international driver's license is required.

Où est la station de taxi?
/u ɛ la stɑsjɔ̃ d taksi/
   Where is the taxi stand?

Où est le bus pour le centre ville?
/u ɛ l(ə) bys pur lə sɑ̃trə vil/
   Where is the bus for the center of town?

Où puis-je louer une voiture?
/u pɥi ʒ lwe yn vwatyːr/
   Where can I rent a car?

■ **En taxi**   *In the taxi*

REMARQUES

The taxi driver will not pick up your luggage or take it into the hotel. He will help you put it in the trunk and take it out. There is a minimum charge which varies according to the city you are in, and you must pay extra for luggage. (These prices are usually posted inside the taxi.) In addition you must tip between 10 and 15%. French taxi drivers are generally talkative and enjoy sharing their opinions about politics or America.

Appelez-moi un taxi, s'il vous plaît.
/aple   mwa ɶ̃ taksi si(l) vu   plɛ/
Call me a cab, please.

Madame, vous devez aller à la station un peu plus loin et
/madam vu   dəvez‿ale a la stɑsjɔ̃ ɶ̃ pø ply lwɛ̃ e

faire la queue.
fɛːr la kø/
You have to go to the taxi stand a bit further on and wait in line.

Chauffeur, conduisez-moi à cette addresse/à l'hôtel.../en ville.
/ʃofœːr   kɔ̃dɥize mwa a sɛt adrɛs   a lotɛl   ɑ̃ vil/
Driver, take me to this address/to the Hotel . . . /in town.

Bien madame.
/bjɛ̃ madam/
O.K.

Pourriez-vous conduire plus lentement, s'il vous plaît.
/purje   vu   kɔ̃dɥːr   ply lɑ̃tmɑ̃   si(l) vu   plɛ/
Could you drive more slowly, please.

C'est loin d'ici, la rue Jacob?
/sɛ   lwɛ̃ disi la ry ʒakɔb/
Is Jacob Street far from here?

Pas très loin. Nous sommes arrivés.
/pɑ trɛ lwɛ̃ nu   sɔmz‿arive/
Not very far. We're here.

C'est combien?
/sɛ kɔ̃bjɛ̃/
How much is it?

Le prix est indiqué au compteur.
/lə pri ɛt‿ɛ̃dike o kɔ̃tœːr/
The price is (indicated) on the meter.

Voilà. Gardez la monnaie.
/vwala garde la mɔnɛ/
Here. Keep the change.

■ **Location de voiture**   *Car rental*

REMARQUES

International car rental firms supply such money- and time-saving extras as airport pick-up and drop-off. The following firms are also located in the United States and reservations may be made in advance.

Avis
26 place Dupleix
Tél: 783–14–75

Eurocar
137 avenue Jean Jaurès
Tél: 645–21–09 Clamart

Hertz
44 rue Emile Deschanel
Tél: 788–37–12 Courbevoie

■ **Aéroports de Paris**   *Paris airports*

93350 – Le Bourget
15kms au nord-est de Paris
Tél: 208-98-90

94310 – Orly
16kms au sud de Paris
Tél: 707-85-55

95500 – Charles de Gaulle (à Roissy en France)
25kms au nord-est de Paris
Tél: 862-12-12

REMARQUES

Bourget and Orly airports have a Paris bus service with offices at Esplanade des Invalides, quai d'Orsay 75007–Paris (tel. 705–82–81)

There is a train service from Orly to Paris-Austerlitz, Pont St-Michel, quai d'Orsay.

From Roissy-Charles de Gaulle there is a direct train service to Porte Maillot (bld. Gouvion St-Cyr) and a bus service (no. 350) to the Gare de l'Est.

Le métro

The Subway

REMARQUES

Each subway line is designated by a number and by the name of the terminus at each end of the line. The first trains leave at 5:30 A.M; the last trains leave at 12:30 A.M. and arrive at the terminus about 1:15 A.M. The subway is in operation every day. There are two classes, first and second. You may buy individual tickets or a booklet of ten; the tickets are also good on Paris buses. Only one ticket is necessary for the subway, regardless of distance traveled or transfers. (The sign for *transfers* is **Correspondances**.) It is wise to keep your ticket until you leave the subway, in case of ticket checks.

There are special four- or seven-day tourist tickets for foreigners which provide unlimited first-class travel by subway, train, or bus. These tickets may be bought at:

L'Office de Tourisme de Paris
127 Champs Elysées
75008 – Paris

Service Touristique de la R.A.T.P.
53 bis quai des Grands Augustins
75006 – Paris

Thirty subway stations (list in each station)

S.N.C.F. stations in Paris (6)

Où est la station de métro?
/u ɛ la stɑsjɔ̃ d metro/
   Where is the subway station?

Il y en a une boulevard Montparnasse.
/i(l) j ãn‿a yn bulvaːr   mɔ̃parnas/
> There is one at Boulevard Montparnasse.

Ce n'est pas trop loin?
/sə n ɛ pɑ tro lwɛ̃/
> It isn't too far?

A deux rues d'ici. J'y vais aussi.
/a dø   ry d isi ʒ i vɛ(z) osi/
> Two blocks from here. I'm going there too.

Cette ligne va à la Place de l'Opéra?
/sɛt   liɲ va a la plas   d(ə) l ɔpera/
> Does that line go to the Place de l'Opéra?

Il   faut prendre une correspondance.
/i(l) fo   prɑ̃dr   yn kɔrɛspɔ̃dɑ̃ːs/
> You have to change.

Où faut-il changer?
/u fot‿i(l) ʃɑ̃ʒe/
> Where do I have to change?

A la station du Châtelet.
/a la stɑsjɔ̃   dy ʃɑtlɛ/
> At the Châtelet station.

La bouche de métro, c'est là-bas?
/la buʃ   də metro s ɛ la bɑ/
> Is the subway entrance down there?

Oui, en face du bureau de tabac.
/wi ã fas dy byro   t taba/
> Yes, opposite the tobacco stand.

Vous avez déjà votre ticket?
/vuz‿ave   deʒa vɔt(r) tikɛ/
> *Do you have your ticket (already)?*

Non, je vais l'acheter.
/nɔ̃   ʒ(ə) vɛ laʃte/
> *No, I'm going to buy it.*

Vous prenez un ticket de première?
/vu   prəne œ̃ tikɛ d(ə) prəmjɛːr/
> *Are you going to get a first-class ticket?*

Oui. Il y a toujours une place assise.
/wi   i(l) j a tuʒuːr   yn plas asiz/
> *Yes. There's always a seat there.*

Vous avez raison.
/vuz‿ ave rezɔ̃/
> *You're right.*

Dépêchons-nous. Voilà le métro.
/depɛʃɔ̃   nu   vwala l(ə) metro/
> *Let's hurry. There's the train.*

L' autobus

The Bus

REMARQUES
    There are regular and double-decker buses in service. Tickets may be bought at subway stations, at bus terminals, in café-tabac stores bearing the red circular R.A.T.P. sign or on the bus. You are charged according to the distance traveled, but within the city limits, the fare is never more than two tickets. Most buses operate from 7 A.M. to 8:30 P.M. A few run as late as 12:30 A.M. and operate on Sundays and holidays. The bus system is also widely used for excursions outside of Paris.

L'autobus s'arrête ici, n'est-ce pas?
/l otɔbys s arɛːt isi n ɛ s pɑ/
    The bus stops here, doesn't it?

Quel autobus voulez-vous prendre?
/kɛl otɔbys vule   vu prɑ̃ːdr/
    Which bus do you want to take?

Celui qui va à la Place de l'Opéra.
/səlɥi ki va a la plas   d(ə) l ɔpera/
    The one that goes to the Place de l'Opéra.

Il   s'arrête ici.
/i(l) s arɛːt   isi/
    It stops here.

Combien de temps faut-il attendre?
/kɔ̃bjɛ̃   d tɑ̃   fot‿il atɑ̃ːdr/
How long do we have to wait?

Il   y en a un toutes les quinze minutes.
/i(l) j ɑ̃n‿a œ̃ tut   le kɛ̃ːz   minyt/
There's one every fifteen minutes.

Combien faut-il de tickets?
/kɔ̃bjɛ̃   fot‿il də tikɛ/
How many tickets do I need?

Un seul ticket est suffisant.
/œ̃ sœl tikɛ ɛ syfizɑ̃/
One ticket's enough.

Faut-il changer de   bus?
/fot‿il ʃɑ̃ʒe   d(ə) bys/
Do we have to change buses?

Non, la ligne est directe.
/nɔ̃   la liɲ ɛ dirɛkt/
No, it's direct.

Dans combien de temps serons-nous à l'Opéra?
/dɑ̃ kɔ̃bjɛ̃   d tɑ̃   srɔ̃   nu a l ɔpera/
How long will it take to get to the Opéra?

Dans quinze minutes, s'il n'y a pas de circulation.
/dɑ̃ kɛ̃ːz   minyt   si(l) n j a pɑ d sirkylasjɔ̃/
Fifteen minutes, if there isn't any traffic.

Et aux heures de pointe?
/e oz‿œːr   də pwɛ̃t/
What about the rush hour?

Cela peut prendre une heure.
/səla pø   prãdr   yn   œːr/
It can take an hour.

J'aime mieux prendre le métro.
/ʒ ɛm   mjø   prãːdr   lə metro/
I prefer to take the subway.

REMARQUES

Additional vocabulary for traveling by bus: **le tramway**
/tramwɛ/, *streetcar*; **le dernier arrêt** /dɛrnje arɛ/, *last stop*; **s'arrêter**
/sarɛte/, *to stop*; **il est défendu de fumer** /il ɛ defãdy d(ə) fyme/,
smoking is not allowed.

descendre /desãːdr/, *to get out or off*; **la fin de section** /fɛ̃ də
sɛksjɔ̃/, *end of zone*; **le terminus** /tɛrminys/, *end of the line*; **un carnet
de tickets** /karnɛ də tikɛ/, *book of tickets*; **détacher** /detaʃe/, *to tear
off.*

Le train

The Train

REMARQUES

The S.N.C.F. is the national railroad company in France. The trains are fast and on time. There are two classes; first, which is more comfortable, and second. The trains may be either **omnibus** stopping at each station or **express ou rapides** stopping at major stations only. The expresses are part of T.E.E. (Trans Europe Express) and stop only a few minutes in big cities; however, you must reserve in advance and pay extra.

The following reductions are in effect:

20% for a round-trip ticket, minimum 5 days (good for 2 months)
30% for a group of 10; 40% for a group of 25 reserved 24 hours in advance (good for 2 months)
50% for a pass to travel all over France for 3 months
20% for weekend pass.

If you plan to travel extensively by train in France or Europe, the best solution is to get a Eurail pass which may be obtained through travel agencies in the U.S.

■ **Gares S.N.C.F. à Paris**   *Train stations in Paris*

Gare de l'Est: région est: Strasbourg, Alsace, Vosges, Allemagne, Suisse.

Gare du Nord: région nord: Lille, Amiens, Belgique, Angleterre, Allemagne.

Gare de Lyon: région sud-est: Lyon, Marseille, Italie, Suisse, Yougoslavie, Grèce.

Gare St-Lazare: région nord-ouest: Rouen, Deauville, Cherbourg, ferryboat vers la Grande-Bretagne.

Gare Montparnasse: région ouest: Le Mans, Brest, Nantes, Bretagne.

Gare d'Austerlitz: région centre et sud-ouest: Bordeaux, Toulouse, Montpellier, Espagne.

Bureau central de renseignements S.N.C.F.: 522-94-00

■ **Pour acheter un billet**   *Buying a ticket*

Monsieur, je voudrais un aller/un aller-retour Paris–Marseille.
/məsjø   ʒə vudrɛ(z) œ̃n‿ale /œ̃n‿ale r(ə)tur pari   marsɛːj/
   I'd like a one-way ticket/a round-trip ticket for Paris–Marseille.

En première ou en deuxième classe?
/ã prəmjɛr u ã døzjɛm   klɑs/
   First or second class?

Quelle est la différence de prix?
/kɛl   ɛ la diferã   də pri/
   What's the difference in price?

A peu près 35% plus cher en première classe.
/a pø prɛ trãtsɛ̃ pur sã ply ʃɛr ã prəmjɛr klɑs/
   About 35% more in first class.

Donnez-moi un billet de   deuxième classe.
/dɔne   mwa œ̃ bijɛ d(ə) døzjɛm   klɑs/
   Give me a second-class ticket.

A quelle heure part le train?
/a kɛl   œːr   paːr lə trɛ̃/
   What time does the train leave?

Le train part à 11h 15 au quai no. 4.
/lə trɛ̃ paːr a ɔːzˬœr kɛ̃ːz o kɛ nymero katr/
The train leaves at 11:15 on track 4.

A quelle heure arriverons-nous à Marseille?
/a kɛl   œr   arivrɔ̃   nu   a marsɛːj/
What time do we arrive in Marseille?

Vous serez à Marseille à 21h .03
/vu   sre   a marsɛːj   a vɛ̃te ynˬœr trwa/
You'll be in Marseille at 9:03 P.M.

Merci beaucoup monsieur.
/mɛrsi boku   məsjø/
Thank you very much.

Dans le train

In the Train

Pardon. Cette place est occupée?
/pardɔ̃   sɛt plas ɛt‿ɔkype/
> *Excuse me. Is this seat taken?*

Non, monsieur, elle est libre.
/nɔ̃   məsjø   ɛl ɛ liːbr/
> *No, it's unoccupied.*

C'est bien le   train pour Paris?
/s ɛ   bjɛ̃ l(ə) trɛ̃   pur pari/
> *Is this the right train for Paris?*

Oui, c'est l'express pour Paris.
/wi   s ɛ   l ɛksprɛs pur pari/
> *Yes, it's the express train to Paris.*

Peut-on fumer dans ce compartiment?
/pøt‿ɔ̃ fyme dɑ̃   sə kɔ̃partimɑ̃/
> *Is smoking allowed in this compartment?*

Il   n'est pas défendu de   fumer.
/i(l) n ɛ   pɑ defɑ̃dy d(ə) fyme/
> *Smoking is not forbidden.*

La fumée ne vous gêne pas, madame?
/la fyme nə vu   ʒɛːn pɑ madam/
> *The smoke doesn't bother you?*

Pas du tout, monsieur.
/pɑ dy tu   məsjø/
Not at all.

Ah, voilà le contrôleur qui vient.
/ɑ vwala l(ə) kɔ̃trolœːr ki vjɛ̃/
Oh, here comes the conductor.

Vos billets, s'il vous plaît!
/vo bijɛ   si(l) vu   plɛ/
Tickets, please!

Est-ce que je l'ai perdu?
/ɛ s kə ʒ(ə) l e pɛrdy/
Have I lost it?

Le voilà par terre.
/lə vwala par tɛːr/
There it is on the floor.

Oh, comme je suis bête!
/o   kɔm   ʒ(ə) sɥi bɛːt/
Oh, I'm really stupid!

Montrez-le à la gare.
/mɔ̃tre   lə a la gaːr/
Show it at the station.

Pour demander son chemin

Asking the Way

Pardon, monsieur l'agent, où est — ?
/pardɔ̃ məsjø   l aʒɑ̃   u ɛ/
    Excuse me, (officer), where is — ?

Faites attention aux voitures!
/fɛt(z) atɑ̃sjɔ̃   o   vwatyːr/
    Look out for the cars!

Où est l'American Express, s'il vous plaît?
/u ɛ   si(l) vu   plɛ/
    Where is American Express, please?

Vous voulez aller à pied?
/vu   vule(z) ale   a pje/
    Do you want to walk?

Oui, si ce n'est pas trop loin.
/wi si s n ɛ   pɑ tro lwɛ̃/
    Yes, if it's not too far.

A la prochaine rue, tournez à droite.
/a la prɔʃɛn   ry   turne(z) a drwɑt/
    At the next street turn right.

Sur l'avenue de l'Opéra?
/syr l avny   d(ə) l ɔpera/
    On the Avenue de l'Opéra?

C'est ça, et puis tout droit.
/s ɛ sa e pɥi tu   drwa/
  Right, and then straight ahead.

Près de la place de l'Opéra?
/prɛ d(ə) la plas   d(ə) l ɔpera/
  Near the Place de l'Opéra?

Sur la place même, à gauche.
/syr la plas mɛːm a goːʃ/
  Right in the Place, to the left.

Au coin du boulevard des Capucines?
/o kwɛ̃ dy bulvaːr   de kapysin/
  On the corner of the Boulevard des Capucines?

Ah, non, au coin de la rue Scribe.
/ɑ nɔ̃ o kwɛ̃ d(ə) la ry skriːb/
  No, on the corner of Scribe Street.

Bon. Je connais le chemin. Merci.
/bɔ̃   ʒ(ə) kɔnɛ   l(ə) ʃmɛ̃   mɛrsi/
  Fine. I know the way. Thank you.

A votre service.
/a vɔt(r) sɛrvis/
  You're welcome.

REMARQUES

Other helpful expressions: **en face** /ɑ̃ fas/, *opposite*; **de ce
côté** /də sə kote/, *on this side*; **de l'autre côté** /də loːtr kote/, *on the
other side*; **par où va-t-on à la gare** / par u vatɔ̃ a la gaːr/? *how does
one get to the station?* **est-ce bien la direction de** . . . /ɛs bjɛ̃ la dirɛksjɔ̃
də/? *is this the right way to* . . .? **quel est le chemin le plus court (le
plus long) pour aller à** . . . /kɛl ɛ l(ə) ʃ(ə)mɛ̃ l(ə) ply kuːr (lə ply lɔ̃) pur
ale a/? *what is the shortest (longest) way to go* . . .?

3

A l'hôtel et au restaurant

At the Hotel and Restaurant

Logement

Where to Stay

REMARQUES

1. In France *hotels* (**hôtels** /otɛl/m.) are ranked on a scale of 0 – 5 stars, and prices vary according to the category. In every big city you will find American-based hotels. The price is always posted on the door of the room. If you travel in summer (July or August), you should write in advance for reservations.

In smaller towns you will find inns which rent rooms by the day or the week and where you may ask for **demi-pension** (*breakfast and one meal*) or **pension complète** (*breakfast and two meals*).

2. **Auberges de jeunesse** /obɛrʒ də ʒœnɛs/ f. (*youth hostels*) are open in all countries to young people aged fifteen to thirty who have a membership card from the F.U.A.J. (Fédération Unie des Auberges de Jeunesse). Minors need the permission of their parents to obtain a membership card. In general you cannot stay for more than three consecutive nights; if you are taking part in a special program or if the hostel is a vacation center, you may stay three weeks. You should reserve in advance if you plan to stay during the summer.

3. If you choose to go *camping* (**le camping** /kãping/), you may set up your tent in a camping area for which you pay a small fee to cover collective facilities.

■ **Quelques adresses**   *Some addresses*

Fédération Unie des Auberges de Jeunesse
6, rue Mesnil
75116 – Paris
Tél: 874-66-79

ou
41, rue Notre Dame de Lorette
75009 – Paris
Tél: 874-36-46
ou

Ligue Française des Auberges de Jeunesse
38, boulevard Raspail
75007 – Paris
Tél: 548-69-84

Guide annuel de la Fédération Française de Camping et de Caravaning
78, rue de Rivoli
75004 – Paris
Tél: 272-84-08
(indique la liste des terrains homologués)

Office de Tourisme de Paris
127, Champs Elysées
75008 – Paris

Union Touristique « Les amis de la Nature »
groupe France
96, rue Championnet
75018 – Paris
Tél: 606-12-72

La réception

Reception Desk

Nous voudrions une chambre à deux lits.
/nu   vudrijɔ̃   yn   ʃɑ̃br   a dø   li/
We'd like a room with two beds.

Avez-vous réservé?
/ave   vu   rezɛrve/
Do you have a reservation?

Je suis Mme Smith. Je vous ai écrit le mois dernier; voici
/ʒə sɥi   madam smit   ʒ(ə) vuz_e   ekri lə mwɑ dɛrnje   vwasi
la confirmation.
la kɔ̃firmɑsjɔ̃/
*I'm Mrs. Smith. I wrote to you last month; here's the
confirmation.*

Désirez-vous une chambre avec douche/salle de bain?
/dezire   vu   yn   ʃɑ̃br   avɛk duʃ   sal   də bɛ̃/
Would you like a room with a shower/bath?

Avec salle de bain, et surtout une chambre sur la cour/la rue/
/avɛk sal   də bɛ̃   e syrtu   yn   ʃɑ̃ːbr   syr la kuːr la ry
avec vue sur la mer.
avɛk vy   syr la mɛːr/
*With bath and above all a room that overlooks the courtyard/
the street/the sea.*

Bien, madame.
/bjɛ̃   madam/
    Fine.

Y a-t-il l'air conditionné et la télévision dans la chambre?
/j a t il lɛr   kɔ̃disjɔne   e la televizjɔ̃   dɑ̃   la ʃɑ̃ːbr/
    Is there air conditioning and a TV in the room?

Oui, madame. Pouvez-vous remplir cette fiche et signer ici.
/wi   madam ˙   puve   vu   rɑ̃pliːr   sɛt   fiʃ   e siɲe   isi
Combien de temps resterez-vous?
kɔ̃bjɛ̃   t tɑ̃   rɛstəre vu/
    Yes. Would you fill out this form and sign here. How long
    will you be staying?

Nous pensons rester une nuit seulement/une semaine/quelques
/nu   pɑ̃sɔ̃   rɛste yn nɥi sœlmɑ̃   yn səmɛn   kɛlkə
jours.
ʒuːr/
    We only plan on staying a night/a week/a few days.

Quel est le prix de la chambre pour une nuit/une semaine/
/kɛl   ɛ   l(ə) pri d(ə) la ʃɑ̃ːbr   pur yn nɥi yn səmɛn
pour la chambre et le petit déjeuner/pour la demi-pension/
pur   la ʃɑ̃br   e lə pti   deʒœne pur   la dəmi pɑ̃sjɔ̃
pour la pension complète?
pur   la pɑ̃sjɔ̃   kɔ̃plɛt/
    How much is the room for a night/a week/with breakfast/
    with breakfast and one meal/with breakfast and two meals?

Les taxes sont-elles comprises?
/le   taks   sɔ̃t‿ɛl   kɔ̃priz/
    Is tax included?

Non, madame. Vous devez ajouter 15%.
/nɔ̃   madam   vu   dəvez‿aʒute   kɛ̃ːz pur sɑ̃/
    No, ma'am. You have to add 15%.

Pouvons-nous voir   la chambre?
/puvɔ̃   nu   vwaːr la ʃãːbr/
May we see the room?

Certainement; voici la clé, chambre no. 47.
/sɛrtɛnmã   vwasi la kle ʃãbr   nymero karãtsɛt/
Certainly; here's the key — room 47.

■ **Elle ne vous plaît pas**   *You don't like it*

Non, je regrette, elle est trop petite/sombre/bruyante.
/nɔ̃   ʒə r(ə)grɛt ɛl ɛ trɔ ptit   sɔ̃br   brɥijãːt/
No, I'm sorry, it's too small/dark/noisy.

Avez-vous une chambre plus grande/plus confortable/plus
/ave vu   yn ʃãːbr   ply grãd ply kɔ̃fɔrtabl   ply
tranquille avec une plus jolie vue?
trãkil   avɛk yn ply ʒɔli vy/
*Do you have a larger/more comfortable/quieter room with a
nicer view?*

■ **Elle vous plaît**   *You do like it*

Très bien, nous la prenons.
/trɛ bjɛ̃   nu   la prənɔ̃/
Fine, we'll take it.

Pouvez-vous faire monter mes bagages?
/puve vu   fɛːr mɔ̃te   me bagaːʒ/
Could you have my luggage brought up?

Oui, madame. Je vais appeler un chasseur.
/wi   madam   ʒ(ə) vɛz‿aple   œ̃ ʃasœːr/
Yes ma'am. I'll call a porter.

Merci beaucoup.
/mɛrsi boku/
Thank you very much.

Le petit déjeuner

Breakfast

REMARQUES

You may have breakfast in your hotel either in your room or in the dining room, the latter being more expensive. There will certainly be a café near your hotel where you will be well served.

■ **Continental**   *Continental*

Garçon, je voudrais un café au lait.
/garsɔ̃   ʒə vudrɛ(z) œ̃ kafe o lɛ/
Waiter, I'd like a regular coffee.

Désirez-vous des croissants?
/dezire vu   de krwasɑ̃/
Would you like croissants?

Oui et aussi des toasts avec du beurre et de la confiture.
/wi e osi   de tost   avɛk dy bœːr e d la kɔ̃fityːr/
Yes and toast with butter and jam, too.

Et vous monsieur?
/e vu   məsjø/
And for you sir?

Puis-je avoir   un thé au citron/au lait et un petit pain.
/pɥi ʒ avwaːr œ̃ te o sitrɔ̃ o lɛ e œ̃ pti pɛ̃/
May I have tea with lemon/with milk and a roll.

Tout de suite monsieur.
/tu t sɥit məsjø/
> *Right away sir.*

■ **A l'anglaise**   *American*

Je voudrais...
/ʒə vudrɛ/
> *I would like . . .*

un jus d'orange /œ̃ ʒy dɔrɑ̃ːʒ/ *orange juice*
un jus de tomate /œ̃ ʒy d tɔmat/ *tomato juice*
un jus de pamplemousse /œ̃ ʒy d pɑ̃pləmus/ *grapefruit juice*
des oeufs au bacon /dez‿ø o bekœn/ *bacon and eggs*
des oeufs au jambon /dez‿ø o ʒɑ̃bɔ̃/ *ham and eggs*
des oeufs au plat /dez‿ø o pla/ *eggs sunnyside up*
des oeufs brouillés /dez‿ø bruje/ *scrambled eggs*
des céréales chaudes /de sereal ʃod/ *hot cereal*
des céréales froides /de sereal frwad/ *cereal*
de la marmelade d'orange /də la marmələd dɔrɑ̃ːʒ/ *orange marmalade*
du café /dy kafe/ *coffee*
du lait /dy lɛ/ *milk*
du thé /dy te/ *tea*

Départ de l'hôtel

Checking Out of the Hotel

Pouvez-vous préparer ma note s'il vous plaît.
/puve vu   prepare ma nɔt si(l) vu   plɛ/
Could you make up my bill please.

Bien, monsieur. Quand partez-vous?
/bjɛ̃ məsjø   kɑ̃   parte vu/
Fine, sir. When are you leaving?

Demain matin vers dix heures.
/d(ə)mɛ̃ matɛ̃ vɛr diz‿œːr/
Tomorrow morning around ten.

Voulez-vous être réveillés?
/vule   vuz‿ ɛːtr revɛje/
Would you like us to wake you?

Oui, s'il vous plaît, vers 8h 30.
/wi si(l) vu   plɛ vɛr ɥit œr trɑ̃ːt/
Yes please, about eight-thirty.

Avez-vous préparé ma note?
/ave vu   prepare ma nɔt/
Have you made up my bill?

Oui monsieur, la voici.
/wi məsjø   la vwasi/
Yes sir, here it is.

Tout est compris? Les taxes aussi?
/tut‿ɛ   kɔ̃pri   le taks osi/
    Is everything included? Tax too?

Oui monsieur. Faut-il aller chercher vos bagages?
/wi məsjø   fot‿il ale ʃɛrʃe   vo baga:ʒ/
    Yes sir. Should someone go and get your luggage?

Non, je les ai descendus. Pouvez-vous me demander un taxi?
/nɔ̃   ʒə lez‿e desɑ̃dy   puve   vu   mə dmɑ̃de   œ̃ taksi/
    No, I brought it down. Could you call me a taxi?

Vous en trouverez un devant l'hôtel. Désirez-vous un reçu?
/vuz‿ɑ̃   truvre   œ̃ d(ə)vɑ̃ lotel   dezire vu   œ̃ rəsy/
    You'll find one in front of the hotel. Do you want a receipt?

Oui, s'il vous plaît.
/wi   si(l) vu   plɛ/
    Yes please.

■ **Quelques problèmes**   *Some problems*

Je ne trouve plus mes bagages.
/ʒə n truv   ply me baga:ʒ/
    I can't find my luggage.

Je ne suis pas d'accord avec cette note.
/ʒə n sɥi pɑ dakɔr   avek sɛt   nɔt/
    I don't agree with this bill.

Je crois qu'il y a une erreur d'addition.
/ʒə krwa ki(l) j a yn   ɛrœr dadjsɔ̃/
    I believe there's a mistake in the addition.

Les restaurants

Restaurants

REMARQUES

1.   French cuisine is one of the principal attractions of France for many tourists. Prices vary according to region, city, sector of the city, and category. Generally, a menu with prices is posted at the entrance to the restaurant. You will also find some restaurants have tourist menus at a flat rate which includes everything.

If you want a quick, light meal, you will find sandwich places almost everywhere; most cafés serve sandwiches at lunch time or **un plat du jour** /pla dy ʒuːr/ (*a special*) which comes with a glass—or two—of wine.

French restaurants are only open at certain hours, generally from 11:30 A.M. to 2:00 P.M. and from 7:30 P.M. to 10:00 P.M.

2.   Meals in France are true ceremonies, particularly dinner. Do not be too pressed for time! A dinner in a good restaurant may last two or two and a half hours, or even take up the entire evening. It is considered normal to have wine with meals; if you do not drink wine, you may ask for mineral water

3.   In *delicatessens* (**charcutier-traiteur comestibles**/ʃar-kytje trɛtœr kɔmɛstibl/) you will find cold cuts, hors d'œuvres, all kinds of specialties, and even simple meals. However, you cannot eat them there—you must take them out.

4.   For deluxe restaurants, you must phone ahead for reservations. You do not have to make reservations for less expensive restaurants.

Allo. Restaurant Lasserre?
/alo rɛstɔrã   lasɛːr/
> *Hello. Restaurant Lasserre?*

Oui monsieur.
/wi məsjø/
> *Yes sir.*

Je voudrais réserver une table pour deux personnes.
/ʒə vudrɛ   rezɛrve yn tabl pur dø   pɛrsɔn/
> *I'd like to reserve a table for two.*

Certainement monsieur.
/sɛrtɛnmã   məsjø/
> *Certainly sir.*

Mercredi soir   à huit heures.
/mɛrkrədi swaːr a ɥit œːr/
> *Wednesday night at eight o'clock.*

Bien monsieur. Votre nom je vous prie?
/bjɛ̃ məsjø   vɔtre nɔ̃ ʒə vu   pri/
> *Fine sir. Could you give me your name please?*

M.   Robert Smith.
/məsjø rɔbɛr   smit/
> *Mr. Robert Smith.*

Voulez-vous une table dans la grande salle ou un peu plus
/vule   vu   yn tabl dã   la grãd   sal   u œ̃ pø plyz‿
isolée?
izɔle/
> *Would you like a table in the main dining room or (some-
> where) a bit more secluded?*

Je préférerais isolée.
/ʒə preferərɛ   izɔle/
> *I'd prefer (something) more secluded.*

Très bien monsieur.
/trɛ bjɛ̃ məsjø/
    Very well sir.

Acceptez-vous la carte Master Charge?
/aksɛpte vu   la kart/
    Do you accept Master Charge?

Etes-vous Américain?
/ɛt   vu   amerikɛ̃/
    Are you American?

Oui, monsieur.
/wi   məsjø/
    Yes.

Bien. Nous acceptons Master Charge et Bank of America avec
/bjɛ̃   nuz‿aksɛptɔ̃   e   avɛk
une pièce d'identité.
yn pjɛs d idɑ̃tite/
    Fine. We accept Master Charge and Bank of America with
    identification.

Bon, merci. Alors à mercredi.
/bɔ̃   mɛrsi   alɔːr a mɛrkrədi/
    Good, thank you. We'll be there Wednesday, then.

Au revoir, monsieur.
/ɔ   rəvwaːr məsjø/
    Good-bye, sir.

■ **Sans réservations**   *Without reservations*

Bonsoir. Une table pour quatre personnes.
/bɔ̃swaːr yn   tabl pur   katr(ə) pɛrsɔn/
    Good evening. A table for four.

Bien monsieur. Vous avez une préférence?
/bjɛ̃ məsjø   vuz   ave   yn   preferɑ̃ːs/
> *Fine   sir.   Anywhere   particular   (lit.   " do   you   have   a*
> *preference ")?*

Je ne sais pas.
/ʒə n sɛ pɑ/
> *I don't know.*

Préférez-vous une table près de la fenêtre, dans un coin ou
/prefere vu   yn   tabl   prɛ d la fnɛːtr   dɑ̃z‿ɛ̃   kwɛ̃ u

dehors?
dəɔːr/
> *Do you prefer a table near the window, in a corner, or*
> *outside?*

Je serai
Oh! une table dehors, cela   sera très agréable!
/o yn tabl deɔr   s(ə)la sra trɛz‿agreabl/
> *Oh, a table outside, that will be nice!*

Par ici, s'il vous plaît.
/par isi si(l) vu   plɛ/
> *This way please.*

Nous attendons deux autres personnes qui doivent nous
/nuz‿atɑ̃dɔ̃   døz‿oːtr(ə)   pɛrsɔn   ki dwav   nu

rejoindre.
rəʒwɛ̃ːdr/
> *We're waiting for two other people to (lit. " who should ")*
> *join us.*

Bien. Je vous sers un apéritif en attendant?
/bjɛ̃   ʒ vu   sɛr   ɛ̃ naperitif ɑ̃n‿atɑ̃dɑ̃/
> *Fine.   May I serve you a cocktail while you're waiting?*

Oui, s'il vous plaît.
/wi   si(l) vu   plɛ/
Yes please.

Madame, qu'est-ce que vous prenez?
/madam   k ɛ   s kə vu   prəne/
Madame, what will you have?

Qu'est-ce que vous me proposez?
/k ɛs   kə vu   mə prɔpoze/
What do you have?

Ricard, Cinzano, Dubonnet, vermouth, whisky.
/rikaːr   sinzano   dybɔne   vɛrmut   wiski/

Un whisky avec de la glace.
/œ̃   wiski   avɛk də la glas/
A whisky on the rocks.

Et pour monsieur, ce sera?
/e   pur   məsjø   sə sra/
And for you sir, what will it be?

Un Cinzano.
/œ̃   sinzano/

■ **Carte ou Menu**   *A la carte or menu*

REMARQUES

The **menu** includes an hors d'œuvre, a main dish (meat or fish), a salad, and cheese or dessert, all for a fixed price. Wine is extra.

The **carte** allows you to choose what you wish (e.g., only a main dish and dessert). The prices are noted alongside each dish.

The wine list is separate from the menu.

■ **Hors-d'œuvre** *Hors d'œuvres*

anchois /ɑ̃ʃwa/*m.* anchovy
assiette (*f.*) **de charcuterie** /asjɛt də ʃarkyt(ə)ri/*f.* cold cuts.
champignons /ʃɑ̃piɲɔ̃/*m.* mushrooms
foie gras fwa gra/ goose liver pâté
hareng /arɑ̃/*m.* herring
hors-d'oeuvre variés /ɔr dœːvr varje/ varied hors d'oeuvres
olives /ɔliv/*f.* olives
pâté (*m.*) **de campagne** /pate d kɑ̃paɲ/*f.* country pâté
pâté de foie /pate də fwa/ liver pâté
rillettes /rijɛt/*f.* potted pork, rabbit, etc.
salade (*f.*) **de tomates** /salad də tɔmat/*f.* tomato salad
sardine /sardin/*f.* sardine
saucisson /sosisɔ̃/*m.* sausage
thon (*m.*) **mayonnaise** /tɔ̃ majɔnɛːz/*f.* tuna fish with mayonnaise

■ **Potage** *Soup*

bisque (*m.*) **d'écrevisses** /bisk dekrəvis/*f.* crayfish bisque
bisque de homard /bisk də ɔmaːr/*m.* lobster bisque
bouillon /bujɔ̃/*m.* bouillon
crème (*f.*) **de céleri** /krɛm də selri/*m.* cream of celery
crème de champignons /krɛm də ʃɑ̃piɲɔ̃/ cream of mushroom
crème d'asperges /krɛm daspɛrʒ/*f.* cream of asparagus
consommé /kɔ̃sɔme/*m.* consommé
potage (*m.*) **julienne** /pɔtaʒ ʒyljɛn/ vegetable soup
potage parmentier /pɔtaʒ parmɑ̃tje/ potato soup
soupe (*f.*) **à l'oignon** /sup a lɔɲɔ̃/*m.* onion soup

■ **Oeufs** *Eggs*

œuf à la coque /œf a la kɔk/ soft-boiled egg
œufs brouillés /ø bruje/ scrambled eggs
œuf dur /œf dyr/ hard-boiled egg
œuf sur le plat /œf syr lə pla/ fried egg (sunnyside up)

omelette au lard /(*f.*)ɔmlɛt o laːr/   omelet with bacon
omelette (*f.*) **aux fines herbes**   /ɔmlɛt o finz_ɛrb/   herb omelet

■ **Poissons et coquillages**   *Sea food*

carpe /karp/*f.* carp
coquilles St. Jacques /kɔkij sɛ̃ ʒak/*f.* scallops
brochet /brɔʃɛ/*m.* pike
crabe /krab/*m.* crab
crevette /krəvɛt/*f.* shrimp
espadon /ɛspadɔ̃/*m.* swordfish
hareng /arɑ̃/*m.* herring
homard /ɔmaːr/*m.* lobster
huître /ɥitr/*f.* oyster
langouste /lɑ̃gust/*f.* African lobster
maquereau /makro/*m.* mackerel
merlan /mɛrlɑ̃/*m.* whiting
morue /mɔry/*f.* cod
moule /mul/*f.* mussel
raie /rɛ/*f.* ray
rouget /ruʒɛ/*m.* red mullet
perche /pɛrʃ/*f.* bass
sardines /sardin/*f.* sardines
saumon /somɔ̃/*m.* salmon
sole /sol/*f.* sole
thon /tɔ̃/*m.* tuna
truite /trɥit/*f.* trout

■ **Gibier et volaille**   *Fowl and game*

aile /ɛl/*f.* wing
blanc /blɑ̃/*m.* breast
caille /kaːj/*f.* quail
canard /kanaːr/*m.* duck
cerf /sɛrf/*m.* venison
chapon /ʃapɔ̃/*m.* capon

chevreuil /ʃəvrœːj/*m.* roe
cuisse /kɥis/*f.* leg
dinde /dɛ̃d/*f.* turkey
faisan /fəzɑ̃/*m.* pheasant
lapin /lapɛ̃/*m.* rabbit
lièvre /ljɛːvr/*m.* hare
oie /wa/*f.* goose
perdrix /pɛrdri/*f.* partridge
poulet /pulɛ/*m.* chicken
sanglier /sɑ̃glije/*m.* wild boar

■ **La viande**   *Meat*

REMARQUES

Because cuts of meat are different in France from American ones, it is difficult to give equivalents. Some useful cuts to know are:

beef   **filet** /filɛ/*m.*
        filet mignon /filɛ miɲɔ̃/
        chateaubriand /ʃɑtobrijɑ̃/*m.*
lamb   **gigot** (*m.*) **d'agneau** /ʒigo daɲo/*m.* leg of lamb
        côtelettes /kotlɛt/*f.* chops
        carré d'agneau /kare daɲo/*m.* loin
pork   **côte** (*f.*) **de porc** /kot də pɔːr/*m.* chops
        épaule (*f.*) **de porc** /epol də pɔːr/ shoulder

andouille /ɑ̃duːj/*f.* chitlins
agneau /aɲo/ lamb
bœuf /bœf/*m.* beef
cervelle /sɛrvɛl/*f.* brains
cœur /kœːr/*m.* heart
côte de bœuf /kot də bœf/ prime rib roast
côtelette de veau /kotlɛt də vo/*m.* veal cutlet
côtelette de mouton /kotlɛt də mutɔ̃/*m.* mutton chop
filet /filɛ/ tenderloin
foie /fwa/ liver
gigot d'agneau /ʒigo daɲo/ leg of lamb

jambon /ʒɑ̃bɔ̃/ *m.* ham
langue /lɑ̃:g/ *f.* tongue
pieds (*m.*) **de veau** /pje d vo/ calf's feet
porc /pɔːr/ pork
ragoût /ragu/ *m.* stew
riz (*m.*) **de veau** /ri d vo/ sweetbreads
steak haché /stɛk aʃe/ hamburger
tripes /trip/ *f.* tripe
veau /vo/ veal

■ **Légumes** *Vegetables*

artichaut /artiʃo/ *m.* artichoke
asperge /aspɛrʒ/ *f.* asparagus
aubergine /obɛrʒin/ *f.* eggplant
avocat /avoka/ *m.* avocado
betterave /bɛtraːv/ *f.* beet
carotte /karɔt/ *f.* carrot
celeri /selri/ *m.* celery
champignon /ʃɑ̃piɲɔ̃/ mushroom
chicorée /ʃikɔre/ *f.* chicory
chou /ʃu/ *m.* cabbage
chou de Bruxelles /ʃu d brysɛl/ Brussels sprout
chou-fleur /ʃu flœːr/ cauliflower
concombre /kɔ̃kɔ̃ːbr/ *m.* cucumber
courge /kurʒ/ *f.* squash
courgettes /kurʒɛt/ *f.* zucchini
cresson /krɛsɔ̃/ *m.* watercress
endive /ɑ̃div/ *f.* endive
épinard /epinaːr/ *m.* spinach
haricot /ariko/ bean
haricot vert /ariko vɛːr/ string bean
laitue /lɛty/ *f.* lettuce
maïs /majis/ *m.* sweet corn
navet /navɛ/ *m.* turnip
gombo /gɔ̃bo/ *m.* okra
oignon /ɔɲɔ̃/ *m.* onion

patate /patat/*f.* sweet potato
petit pois /pti pwa/ green pea
poireaux /pwaro/*m.* leeks
poivron vert /pwavrɔ̃ vɛːr/ green pepper
pomme (*f.*) **de terre** /pɔm də tɛr/ potato
tomate /tɔmat/ tomato

■ **Fruits** *Fruit*

abricot /abriko/*m.* apricot
ananas /anana(s)/*m.* pineapple
avocat /avoka/ avocado
banane /banan/*f.* banana
cerise /səriz/*f.* cherry
citron /sitrɔ̃/*m.* lemon
datte /dat/*f.* date
figue /fig/*f.* fig
fraise /frɛz/*f.* strawberry
framboise /frɑ̃bwaːz/*f.* raspberry
grenade /grənad/*f.* pomegranate
groseille /grozɛːj/*f.* gooseberry
limon /limɔ̃/*m.* lime
mandarine /mɑ̃darin/*f.* tangerine
melon /məlɔ̃/*m.* melon
mûre /myːr/*f.* blackberry
myrtille /mirtil/*f.* blueberry
orange /ɔrɑ̃ːʒ/*f.* orange
pamplemousse /pɑ̃pləmus/*m.* grapefruit
pastèque /pastɛk/*f.* watermelon
pêche /pɛʃ/*f.* peach
poire /pwaːr/*f.* pear
pomme /pɔm/*f.* apple
prune /pryn/*f.* plum
pruneau /pryno/*m.* prune
raisin /rɛzɛ̃/*m.* grape

raisin sec - raisin

■ Dessert   *Dessert, sweets*

compote   /kɔ̃pɔt/ *f.*   stewed fruit
confiture   /kɔ̃fityːr/ *f.*   preserves
flan   /flã/ *m.*   custard
une **glace**   /glas/ *f.*   ice cream *(u à la vanille· au· glace au chocolat·*
gelée   /ʒəle/ *f.*   jelly
marmelade   /marməlad/ *f.*   marmalade
pâtisserie   /pɑtisri/ *f.*   pastry
sorbet   /sɔrbɛ/ *m.*   sherbet
tarte   /tart/ *f.*   pie
gateau

■ Vous passez la commande   *Ordering*

(Le garçon) Vous avez choisi?
/lə garsɔ̃   vuz‿ave   ʃwazi/
    Have you decided?

Oui; je prendrai un gigot de mouton.
/wi   ʒə prãdre   œ̃   ʒigo d mutɔ̃/
    Yes, I'll have leg of lamb.

Et moi, un filet de sole.
/e mwa œ̃ filɛ   d sol/
    And for me, a filet of sole.

Quels sont les légumes avec le gigot?
/kɛl   sɔ̃   le legym   avɛk lə ʒigo/
    What are the vegetables with the lamb?

(Le garçon) Des haricots verts et des pommes de terre sautées.
    /de ariko   vɛr   e de pɔm   də tɛr   sote/
    Green beans and hash brown potatoes.

Très bien.
/trɛ   bjɛ̃/
    Fine.

apportez-moi — bring me.

(Le garçon) Et comme entrée?
/e kɔm   ãtre/
And for an appetizer?

Je prendrai une salade de tomates.
/ʒə prãdre   yn salad də tɔmat/
I'll have a tomato salad.

(Le garçon) Et pour madame?
/e pur   madam/
And for you ma'am?

Un pâté de foie.
/ɶ̃ pɑte də fwa/
Liver pâté.

(Le garçon) Voulez-vous la carte des vins?
/vule   vu la kart de vɛ̃/
Do you want the wine list?

Merci. Nous voudrions une demi-bouteille de Côtes du Rhône.
/mɛrsi nu   vudrijɔ̃   yn dəmi butɛːj   də kot   dy ron/
Thank you. We'd like half a bottle of Côtes du Rhône.

J'aimerais du vin blanc sec pour mon poisson.
/ʒɛmrɛ   dy vɛ̃ blɑ̃ sɛk pur mɔ̃ pwasɔ̃/
I'd like a dry white wine for the fish.

Pour terminer nous prendrons le plateau de fromages.
/pur tɛrmine nu   prãdrɔ̃   lə plato   d(ə) frɔmaːʒ/
And finally we'll have the cheese selection.

Merci bien.
/mɛrsi bjɛ̃/
Thank you very much.

■ Boissons   *Drinks*

REMARQUES

In France choosing the right wine to accompany a particular dish is regarded as important. For example:

Hors d'œuvres, fish, shellfish, seafood, oysters require dry white wines or champagne brut: Muscadet, Pouilly-Fuissé, Sancerre, dry Vouvray.

Poultry, white meat require light red wines: Beaujolais, Bourgueil, Graves, Médoc.

Red meat, game, cheese require full-bodied red wines: Bordeaux, Châteauneuf-du-Pape, Côtes du Rhône, Pomerol, St.-Emilion.

Desserts, fruits require sweet wines: Anjou, Monbazillac, Sauternes, champagne demi-sec.

alcool /alkɔl/*m*. alcohol

apéritif /aperitif/*m*. apéritif, appetizer

bière /bjɛːr/*f*. beer

bière blonde /blɔ̃d/ light beer

bière brune /bryn/ dark beer

cacao /kakao/*m*. cocoa

café /kafe/*m*. coffee

champagne /ʃɑ̃paɲ/*m*. champagne

chocolat /ʃɔkɔla/*m*. chocolate

cidre /sidr/*m*. cider

cognac /kɔɲak/*m*. brandy, cognac

eau (potable) /o pɔtabl/ (drinking) water

eau gazeuse /gazøz/ charged water

eau minérale /mineral/ mineral water

eau de Seltz /o d(ə) sɛltz/ Seltzer water

eau-de-vie /o d(ə) vi/ brandy

gin /dʒin/*m*. gin

lait /lɛ/*m*. milk

lait pasteurisé /pastœrize/ pasteurized milk

limonade /limɔnad/*f*. lemonade

liqueur /likœːr/*f*. liqueur

orangeade /ɔrɑ̃ʒad/*f*. orangeade

Porto /pɔrto/*m*. port wine

rafraîchissement /rafrɛʃismɑ̃/*m*. refreshment

rhum /rɔm/*m*. rum

thé /te/*m*. tea

vin /vɛ̃/*m*. wine

vin blanc /blɑ̃/ white wine

vin de Bordeaux /vɛ̃ d(ə) bɔrdo/ Bordeaux wine

vin de Bourgogne /vɛ̃ d(ə) burgɔɲ/ Burgundy wine

vin mousseux /musø/ spark-
    ling wine
vin rosé /roze/   rosé wine

vin rouge /ruːʒ/   red wine
Xérès /kserɛs/*m.*   sherry

■ Comment l'aimez-vous?   *How do you like it?*

	Fish **Poisson**	*Meat* **Viande**	*Vegetables* **Légumes**
baked	cuit au four /kɥi/	cuite au four	cuits au four
barbecued		à la broche /a la brɔʃ/	
boiled	bouilli /buji/	bouillie	bouillis
braised		braisée /breze/	
broiled	grillé /grije/	grillée	grillés
chopped		hachée /aʃe/	
creamed			à la crème /a la krɛm/
fried	frit /fri/	frite	frits
marinated	mariné /mariné/	marinée	
mashed			en purée /ã pyre/
medium		à point /a pwɛ̃/	
pickled			marinés
rare		saignante /sɛɲãːt/	
raw	cru /kry/	crue	crus
roasted		rôtie /roti/	

smoked	fumé /fyme/	fumée
steamed		à la vapeur /a la vapœːr/
stewed	en ragoût /ɑ̃ ragu/	en ragoût
well done		bien cuite /bjɛ̃ kɥit/

■ **Petit lexique pour gourmets**   *Brief gourmet glossary*

aiguillette de caneton or **de canard**   /egɥijɛt də kantɔ̃ də kanaːr/
thin, tender slice of duckling, cut lengthwise

aïoli   /ajɔli/   garlic-spiced mayonnaise, usually served with fish or
cold meat

andouillette ˈ /ɑ̃dujɛt/   sausage made of pork or veal tripe

ballottine   /balɔtin/   a variety of galantine (white meat molded in
aspic)

bar   /bar/   sea bass (see *loup au fenouil* below)

barbue   /barby/   brill

béarnaise   /bearnɛz/   sauce made of butter, eggs, tarragon,
vinegar and lemon juice, served with steaks and some fish
dishes

belons   /bəlɔ̃/   variety of flat oyster with delicate flavor

beurre blanc   /bœr blɑ̃/   " white butter," a creamy sauce made of
butter well whipped with vinegar and shallots, served with pike
and other fish

bœuf à la ficelle   /bœf a la fisɛl/   " beef on a string," piece of fillet
of beef tied with string and plunged for a very short time in
boiling meat stock

Bordelaise (à la)   /bɔrdəlɛz (a la)/   red wine sauce with shallots
and bone marrow

boudin grillé   /budɛ̃ grije/   grilled pork blood sausage

bouillabaisse   /bujabɛs/   soup of fish and, sometimes, shellfish,
cooked with garlic, parsley, tomatoes, olive oil, spices, onions,
and saffron. The fish and the soup are served separately. A
Marseille specialty

bourride /burid/ fish chowder prepared with white fish, garlic, spices, herbs and white wine, served with *aïoli* (see above)

brochette (en) /brɔʃɛt (ã)/ skewered

canard à l'orange /kanar a lɔrã:ʒ/ roast duck with orange

canard aux olives /kanar oz‿ɔliv/ roast duck with olives

caneton au cidre /kantɔ̃ o sidr/ duckling cooked in cider

canette au vinaigre de Xérès /kanɛt o vinɛgr də kserɛs/ young female duck cooked in sherry vinegar

carré d'agneau /kare daɲo/ rack of lamb (loin chops)

cassoulet /kasulɛ/ casserole dish made of white beans, condiments, served (depending on the recipe) with sausage, pork, mutton, goose, or duck

cèpes /sɛp/ kind of mushroom

charcuterie d'Auvergne /ʃarkytri dovɛrɲ/ a region of central France, Auvergne is reputed to produce the best country-prepared pork-meat specialties, served cold as a first course

chateaubriand /ʃɑtobrijã/ thick, tender cut of steak from the heart of the fillet or tenderloin

chevreuil /ʃəvrœ:j/ venison

chou farci /ʃu farsi/ stuffed cabbage

choucroute garnie /ʃukrut garni/ sauerkraut, an Alsatian specialty, served hot and " garnished " with ham, frankfurters, bacon, smoked pork, sausage, and boiled potatoes. A good dish to order in a *brasserie*

civet de gibier /sivɛ d(ə) ʒibje/ game stew with wine and onions (*civet de lièvre* = jugged hare)

civet de porcelet /sivɛ d(ə) pɔrsəlɛ/ jugged piglet

confit de canard or **d'oie** /kɔ̃fi d kana:r dwa/ preserved duck or goose cooked in its own fat (sometimes served with *cassoulet*, see above)

coq au vin /kɔk o vɛ̃/ chicken (lit. " rooster ") cooked in red wine sauce with onions, mushrooms, and bits of bacon

coquilles St-Jacques /kɔkij sɛ̃ ʒak/ scallops

côte de bœuf /kot də bœf/ roast ribs of beef

côte de veau /kot də vo/ veal chop

cou d'oie farci /ku dwa farsi/ stuffed goose neck

coulis /kuli/ thick sauce

couscous /kuskus/ north African dish of semolina (crushed wheat grain) steamed and served with a broth of chickpeas and other vegetables, a spicy sauce, accompanied by chicken, skewered lamb, or sausage

crêpes /krɛp/ thin, light pancakes

daube (bœuf en) /dob (bœf ã)/ beef braised with carrots and onions in red wine sauce

délices de Bourgogne /delis də burgɔɲ/ see snails under *escargots*

écrevisses /ekrəvis/ freshwater crayfish

entrecôte marchand de vin /ãtrəkot mãrʃã d(ə) vɛ̃/ rib steak in a red wine sauce with shallots

escalope de veau /ɛskalɔp də vo/ (thin) veal steak, sometimes served *panée*, breaded, as with *Wiener Schnitzel*

escargots /ɛskargo/ snails, usually prepared with butter, garlic, and parsley

feuilleté /fœjte/ flaky puff pastry used for making meat and fish pies or cheese and fruit tarts

filet de bœuf /filɛ d bœf/ fillet (tenderloin) of beef

filets de sole /filɛ d sol/ fillets of sole

filet mignon /miɲɔ̃/ small, round, very choice cut of beef from the tenderloin

flambé (e) /flãbe/ " flamed," i.e., bathed in brandy, rum, etc., which is then ignited

foie gras d'oie or **de canard** /fwa gra dwa də kanar/ liver of fatted geese or ducks, served fresh (*frais*) or in *pâté* (see below)

foie de veau /fwa d vo/ calf's liver

fricassée de poulet aux morilles /frikase d pulɛ o mɔril/ chicken fricassee with morel mushrooms

garbure /garbyːr/ kind of cabbage soup from the southwest of France

gibier /ʒibje/ game

grand veneur /grã vnœːr/ rich sauce served with game, made of the blood of the game marinated with vinegar, white wine, crushed peppercorns, etc.

gratin (au) /gratɛ̃ (o)/ dish baked in the oven to produce thin crust on surface

gratinée /gratine/   see onion soup under *soupe à l'oignon*
grenouilles (cuisses de) /grənuːj (kɥis də)/   frogs' legs, often served
  à la provençale (see below)
grillades /grijad/   broiled meats, mostly steaks

homard à l'américaine or **à l'armoricaine** /ɔmar a lamerikɛn a
  larmɔrikɛn/   lobster sautéed in butter and olive oil, served
  with a sauce composed of tomatoes, garlic, onion, spices, white
  wine, and cognac

lamproie /lãprwa/   lamprey, often served *à la bordelaise* (see
  above)
langoustines /lãgustin/   large prawns
lièvre /ljɛːvr/   hare (for *civet de lièvre*, see above)
loup au fenouil /lu o fənuːj/   in the south of France, see bass with
  fennel (same as *bar*)

magret /magrɛ/   duck steak
marcassin /markasɛ̃/   young wild boar
marmite dieppoise /marmit djɛpwaːz/   fish soup from Dieppe
matelote d'anguilles /matlɔt dãgiːj/   eel stew with red wine,
  onions, and herbs
merlan /mɛrlã/   whiting, a fish related to the cod
moelle (à la) /mwal (a la)/   with bone marrow
moules farcies /mul farsi/   stuffed mussels (usually filled with
  butter, garlic, and parsley)
moules marinières /marinjɛːr/   mussels steamed in their shells,
  together with white wine, onions, and spices

nantua /nãtɥa/   sauce made with freshwater crayfish tails and
  served with *quenelles*, fish, seafood, etc.
navarin /navarɛ̃/   lamb stew with small onions, carrots, turnips,
  and potatoes
noisettes d'agneau /nwazɛt daɲo/   small, round, choice morsels
  of lamb
œufs en meurette /ø ã mœrɛt/   poached eggs in red wine sauce
  with bits of bacon

paëlla /paɛja/   a saffron-flavored rice dish made with a mixture
  of seafood, sausage, chicken, and vegetables

pâté /pɑte/   also called terrine. A common French hors d'œuvre, a kind of cold, sliced meat loaf which is made from pork, veal, liver, fowl, rabbit or game and seasoned appropriately with spices. Also served hot in pastry crust (*en croûte*)

paupiette /popjɛt/   usually, slice of veal wrapped around pork or sausage meat

pavé Villette /pave vilɛt/   a *Chateaubriand* steak, so called after the famous Paris slaughterhouse district

perdreau /pɛrdro/   young partridge

petit salé /pti sale/   salt pork tenderloin, usually served with lentils or cabbage

petits gris /pti gri/   literally, " small grays "; a variety of snail with brownish, pebbled shell

pétoncles farcies /petɔ̃klə farsi/   small scallops prepared with butter, garlic, and parsley

pieds de mouton Poulette /pje d mutɔ̃ pulɛt/   sheep's feet in cream sauce

pintade /pɛ̃tad/   guinea fowl

piperade /piprad/   kind of Spanish omelette, a Basque dish of scrambled eggs and cooked tomato, green pepper, and Bayonne ham

plateau de fromages /plato d(ə) frɔmaːʒ/   tray with a selection of cheeses made from cow's or goat's milk

pot-au-feu /pɔt o fø/   beef soup which is served first and followed by a joint of beef cooked in the soup, garnished with vegetables

poularde aux concombres /pulard o kɔ̃kɔ̃ːbr/   young fattened chicken with cucumber

poule du bon roy Henry, or **poule au pot** /pul dy bɔ̃ rwa ɑ̃ri pul o po/   " Good King Henry's chicken in the pot ": the hot broth is eaten first, then the boiled chicken and vegetables

poulet de Bresse /pulɛ d brɛs/   finest breed of chicken in France, grain-fed

poulet à l'estragon /pulɛ a lɛstragɔ̃/   chicken with tarragon

poulet sauté vallée d'Auge /sote vale doʒ/   chicken sautéed in cream sauce with Calvados (apple brandy from Normandy)

poulet aux écrevisses /pulɛ oz‿ekrəvis/   chicken with crayfish

pré salé   /pre sale/   a particularly fine variety of lamb raised on salt marshes near the sea

provençale (à la)   /prɔvãsal (a la)/   with garlic and parsley

quenelles de brochet   /kənɛl də brɔʃɛ/   fishballs made of pike; *quenelles* are also made of veal or chicken forcemeat

quiche lorraine   /kiʃ lɔrɛn/   hot custard pie flavored with chopped bacon and baked in an unsweetened pastry shell

raie aux câpres   /rɛ o kɑːpr/   skate fried in butter garnished with capers

St-Pierre   /sɛ̃ pjɛːr/   John Dory

salade niçoise   /salad niswaːz/   a first course made of lettuce, tomatoes, celery, olives, green pepper, cucumber, anchovy, and tuna, seasoned to taste.   A favorite hors d'œuvre

saucisson chaud   /sosisɔ̃ ʃo/   pork sausage, served hot with potato salad, or sometimes in pastry shell (*en croûte*)

saumon fumé   /somɔ̃ fyme/   smoked salmon

scampi fritti   /skãpi friti/   French-fried shrimp

selle d'agneau   /sɛl daɲo/   saddle of lamb

soufflé   /sufle/   a light, fluffy baked dish made of egg yolks and whites beaten separately and combined with cheese or fish, for example, to make a first course, or with fruit or liqueur as a dessert

soupe de poissons   /sup də pwasɔ̃/   fish chowder

steak au poivre   /stɛk o pwaːvr/   pepper steak, often served flamed

suprême   /syprɛm/   usually refers to poultry or fish served with a white sauce

terrine   /tɛrin/   see above under *pâté*

tournedos   /turnədo/   small, round tenderloin steak

truffe   /tryf/   truffle

truite   /trɥit/   trout

vol-au-vent   /vɔl o vã/   puff pastry shell filled with chicken, meat, fish, fishballs (*quenelles*) usually in cream sauce with mushrooms

Desserts

baba au rhum /baba o rɔm/   sponge cake soaked in rum, sometimes served with whipped cream
beignets de pommes /bɛɲɛ d pɔm/   apple fritters
clafoutis /klafuti/   dessert of apples (cherries, or other fruit) baked in batter
glace /glas/   ice cream
pâtisseries /pɑtisri/   pastry, cakes
profiteroles /prɔfitrɔl/   small round pastry puffs filled with ice cream and covered with chocolate sauce
St-Honoré /sɛ̃t ɔnɔre/   cake made of two kinds of pastry and whipped cream, named after the patron saint of pastry cooks
tarte aux pommes /tart o pɔm/   open apple tart
tarte tatin /tart tatɛ̃/   apple upside-down cake, caramelized and served hot
vacherin /vaʃrɛ̃/   meringue with ice cream and whipped cream

■ **L'addition**   *The bill*

L'addition, s'il vous plaît.
/ladisjɔ̃   si(l) vu   plɛ/
   Check please.

Certainement, monsieur.
/sɛrtɛnmɑ̃   məsjø/
   Certainly, sir.

Est-ce que le service est compris?
/ɛs   kə   l(ə) sɛrvis   ɛ   kɔ̃pri/
   Is the tip included?

Oui monsieur.
/wi   məsjø/
   Yes sir.

Le dîner était délicieux.
/lə dine etɛ delisjø/
> *The dinner was delicious.*

Puis-je payer en dollars?
/pɥiʒ pɛje ɑ̃ dɔlar/
> *Can I pay with dollars?*

Non monsieur, je regrette.
/nɔ̃ məsjø   ʒə r(ə)grɛt/
> *No sir, I'm sorry.*

■ **Quelques problèmes**   *Some problems*

Ma viande est trop cuite/trop saignante/dure/crue.
/ma vjɑ̃d ɛ tro kɥit tro sɛɲɑ̃ːt   dyr kry/
> *My meat is overdone/too rare/tough/raw.*

Le vin blanc n'est pas assez froid.
/lə vɛ̃ blɑ̃ nɛ pɑ(z)ase frwa/
> *The white wine isn't cold enough.*

Ce poisson n'est pas frais.
/sə pwasɔ̃ nɛ pɑ frɛ/
> *This fish isn't fresh.*

Nous attendons depuis une demi-heure.
/nuz‿atɑ̃dɔ̃   dəpɥi yn dəmi œːr/
> *We've been waiting for half an hour.*

C'est trop sucré/salé.
/sɛ tro sykre sale/
> *It's too sweet/salty.*

4

Les achats et les services

Shopping and Services

Les achats

Shopping

REMARQUES

Store hours vary greatly in France. Food stores are open from 9 A.M. to 1 P.M. and from 4 P.M. to 7 P.M.

chez le boulanger   *boulanger - baker*

bakery **boulangerie** /bulɑ̃ʒri/ *f.*
butcher shop **boucherie** /buʃri/ *f.*
candy store **confiserie** /kɔ̃fizri/ *f.*
dairy store **crêmerie-laiterie** /krɛmrti lɛtri/ *f.*
delicatessen **charcuterie-comestibles** /ʃarkytri kɔmɛstibl/ *f.*
fish store **poissonnerie** /pwasɔnri/ *f.*
fruit and vegetables market **boutique** (*f.*) **de fruits et légumes** /butik d frɥi e legym/
grocery store **épicerie** /episri/ *f.*
liquor store **vin et liqueurs** /vɛ̃ e likœːr/

You can find nearly everywhere *supermarkets*—**supermarchés à l'américaine**—where you can buy everything at good prices. Some major supermarkets are Carrefour, C et A. Mamouth.

In cities you will find *department stores* (**grands magasins** m.) such as: Monoprix, Prisunic, Printemps, Galeries Layfayette, Inno, and Samaritaine. These stores are open from 9 A.M. to 7 P.M. and some evenings until 10:00.

■ **Boutiques**   *Small stores*

antique store **magasin** (*m.*) **d'antiquités** /magazɛ̃ dɑ̃tikite/ *f.*
book store **librairie** /librɛri/ *f.*

camera store **magasin de photo** /magazɛ̃ d fɔto/
florist **fleuriste** /flœrist/ *m.*
furrier **fourreur** /furœːr/ *m.*
jeweller **bijoutier** /biʒutje/ *f.*
launderette **salon lavoir** /salɔ̃ lavwaːr/ *m.*
leather goods store **maroquinerie** /marɔkinri/ *f.*
optician **opticien** /ɔptisjɛ̃/ *m.*
record store **disquaire** /diskɛːr/ *m.*
sewing store **mercerie** /mɛrsri/ *f.*
shirt maker **chemiserie** /ʃəmizri/ *f.*
shoe store **magasin de chaussures** /magazɛ̃ d(ə) ʃosyːr/
sporting goods store **magasin d'articles de sport** /magazɛ̃ dartikl
   də spɔːr/
stationery store **papèterie** /papɛtri/ *f.*
tailor **tailleur** /tɑjœːr/ *m.*
tobacco store **bureau de tabac** /byro d taba/ *m.*
watchmaker **horloger** /ɔrlɔʒe/ *m.*

■ **Services** *Services*

bank **banque** /bɑ̃k/ *f.*
dentist **dentiste** /dɑ̃tist/ *m.*
doctor **médecin** /medsɛ̃/ *m.*
drugstore **pharmacie** /farmasi/ *f.*
dry cleaner **teinturerie** /tɛ̃tyrəri/ *f.*
garage **garage** /garaːʒ/ *m.*
gas station **station service** /stɑsjɔ̃ sɛrvis/ *f.*
hospital **hôpital** /ɔpital/ *m.*
laundry **blanchisserie** /blɑ̃ʃisri/ *f.*
police station **poste de police** /pɔst də pɔlis/ *m.*
post office **PTT — poste-télégraphe-téléphone** /pɔst telegraf
   telefɔn/ *f.*
shoemaker **cordonnier** /kɔrdɔnje/ *f.*
travel agency **agence de voyage** /aʒɑ̃s də vwajaːʒ/ *f.*

■ Taille   *Sizes*

Dames   *Women*

robes/ensembles   dresses/suits

Europe	38	40	42	44	46	48
America	10	12	14	16	18	20

bas/collants   hose/pantyhose

Europe	0	1	2	3	4	5
America	8	8½	9	9½	10	10½

Messieurs   *Men*

costumes/pardessus   suits/coats

Europe	46	48	50	52	54
America	36	38	40	42	44

chemises   shirts

Europe	36	38	41	43	45
America	14	15	16	17	18

■ Vêtements   *Clothing*

bathrobe   **robe de chambre**   /rɔb də ʃɑ̃ːbr/   *f.*
bathing cap   **bonnet de bain**   /bɔnɛ d bɛ̃/   *m.*
bathing suit   **maillot de bain**   /majo d bɛ̃/   *m.*
belt   **ceinture**   /sɛ̃tyːr/   *f.*
bikini   **bikini**   /bikini/   *m.*
blazer   **blazer**   /blazɛr/   *m.*
blouse   **blouse**   /bluz/   *f.*
bow tie   **nœud papillon**   /nø papijɔ̃/   *m.*
bra   **soutien-gorge**   /sutjɛ̃ gɔrʒ/   *m.*
briefs   **slip**   /slip/   *m.*
cap   **bonnet** (*m.*)/**casquette**   /bɔnɛ/kaskɛt/   *f.*
cardigan   **cardigan**   /kardigɑ̃/   *m.*
coat   **manteau**   /mɑ̃to/   *m.*

dress **robe** /rɔb/ *f.*
evening dress **robe du soir** /rɔb dy swaːr/
fur coat **manteau de fourrure** /mãto d(ə) furyːr/ *m.*
girdle **gaine** /gɛn/ *f.*
gloves **gants** /gã/ *m.*
handkerchief **mouchoir** /muʃwaːr/ *m.*
hat **chapeau** /ʃapo/ *m.*
jacket **veston** /vɛstɔ̃/ *m.*
jersey **pull** /pyl/ *m.*
jumper **tricot** /triko/ *m.*
lingerie **lingerie** /lɛ̃ʒri/ *f.*
necktie **cravate** /kravat/ *f.*
negligee **négligé** /negliʒe/ *m.*
nightgown **chemise de nuit** /ʃəmiz də nɥi/ *f.*
overalls **salopette** /salɔpɛt/ *f.*
overcoat **pardessus** /pardəsy/ *m.*
pajamas **pyjama** /piʒama/ *m.*
panties **slip** /slip/ *m.*
pants **pantalon** /pãtalɔ̃/ *m.*
panty girdle **gaine-culotte** /gɛn kylɔt/ *f.*
panty hose **collant** /kɔlã/ *m.*
raincoat **imperméable** /ɛ̃pɛrmeabl/ *m.*
robe **peignoir** /pɛɲwaːr/ *m.*
sandals **sandales** /sãdal/ *f.*
scarf **foulard** /fulaːr/ *m.*
shirt **chemise** /ʃəmiz/ *f.*
shoes **chaussures** /ʃosyːr/ *f.*
gym shoes **chaussures (*f.*) de gymnastique** /ʃosyr də ʒimnastik/
tennis shoes **chaussures de tennis** /ʃosyr də tɛnis/
shorts **shorts** /ʃɔrt/ *m.*
skirt **jupe** /ʒyp/ *f.*
slippers **pantoufles** /pãtufl/ *f.*
sneakers **espadrilles** /ɛspadriːj/ *f.*
socks **chaussettes** /ʃosɛt/ *f.*
sports jacket **veste de sport** /vɛst də spɔ̃ːr/ *f.*
stockings **bas** /bɑ/ *m.*
stole **écharpe** /eʃarp/ *f.*
suit (women) **ensemble** /ãsãbl/ *m.*

suit (men)   **costume/complet**   /kɔstym/kɔ̃plɛ/   *m.*
sweater   **chandail**   /ʃɑ̃daːj/   *m.*
sweatshirt   **blouson de sport**   /bluzɔ̃ d(ə) spɔːr/   *m.*
T-shirt   **T-shirt**   /te ʃœrt/   *m.*
track suit   **survêtement**   /syrvɛtmɑ̃/   *m.*
tuxedo   **smoking**   /smɔkiɲ/   *m.*
underpants   **caleçon**   /kalsɔ̃/   *m.*
undershirt   **maillot de corps**   /majo d(ə) kɔːr/

■ **Couleurs**   *Colors*

beige   **beige**   /bɛːʒ/
black   **noir**   /nwaːr/
blue   **bleu**   /blø/
brown   **brun/marron**   /brœ̃/marɔ̃/
green   **vert**   /vɛːr/
grey   **gris**   /gri/
orange   **orange**   /ɔrɑ̃ːʒ/
pink   **rose**   /roːz/
red   **rouge**   /ruːʒ/
violet   **violet**   /vjɔlɛ/
white   **blanc**   /blɑ̃/
yellow   **jaune**   /ʒoːn/

A la boutique

At the Clothing Store

Je voudrais une robe en coton.
/ʒə vudrɛ(z) yn rɔb ɑ̃ kɔtɔ̃/
  I'd like a cotton dress.

Quelle est votre taille?
/kɛl ɛ vɔtr(ə) tɑːj/
  What is your size?

Je ne sais pas exactement. Pouvez-vous prendre mes mesures?
/ʒə n sɛ pɑ ɛgzaktəmɑ̃ puve vu prɑ̃ːdr me məzyːr/
  I don't know exactly. Could you take my measurements?

Vous faites un 38.
/vu fɛt œ̃ trɑ̃t ɥit/
  You take a 38.[1]

Celle-ci est trop foncée. Avez-vous quelque chose de plus
/sɛl si ɛ tro fɔ̃se   ave vu kɛlkə ʃoːz də ply
clair?
klɛːr/
  This one's too dark. Do you have something lighter?

En voici une beige.
/ɑ̃ vwasi yn bɛːʒ/
  Here's a beige one.

[1] This is a European size.

Puis-je l'essayer?
/pɥiʒ   lɛsɛje/
> May I try it on?

La cabine d'essayage est derrière vous. Vous avez une glace.
/la kabin dɛsɛjaʒ   ɛ dɛrjɛr vu   vuz‿ave   yn glas/
> The dressing room's behind you. You'll have a mirror there.

Je crois que cela ne me va pas.
/ʒə krwa kə   sla nə m va pɑ/
> I don't think this looks good on me.

Mais si, cela vous va très bien.
/mɛ si sla vu   va trɛ bjɛ̃/
> But it does; it looks wonderful on you.

Elle est trop courte/longue/serrée/large.
/ɛl ɛ   tro kurt lɔ̃g   sɛre   larʒ/
> It's too short/long/tight/big.

On peut vous faire une retouche.
/ɔ̃ pø vu fɛr yn rətuʃ/
> We can alter it for you.

Combien de temps faut-il attendre?
/kɔ̃bjɛ̃   t tɑ̃   fotil atɑ̃ːdr/
> How long do I have to wait?

Deux ou trois jours.
/dø   u trwa ʒuːr/
> Two or three days.

C'est impossible, je pars demain.
/sɛt‿ɛ̃pɔsibl   ʒə paːr dəmɛ̃/
> That's impossible; I'm leaving tomorrow.

Le chausseur

The Shoe Store

■ **Tailles**   *Sizes*

Women

Europe	36	38	38½	40
America	6	7	8	9

Men

Europe	38	39½	40½	42	42½	43	43½	44	45
America	5	6	7	8	8½	9	9½	10	11

bottes /bɔt/*f.* boots
sandales /sãdal/*f.* sandals
chaussures /ʃosyːr/*f.* shoes
tennis /tɛnis/*m.* sneakers
pantoufles /pãtufl/*f.* slippers

J'aimerais une paire de...
/ʒəmrɛ   yn pɛr   də/
    I would like a pair of . . .

Oui, monsieur. Quelle est votre pointure?
/wi məsjø   kɛl   ɛ   vɔtr(ə) pwɛ̃tyːr/
    Yes, sir. What size do you take?

Sept ou huit je pense.
/sɛt u ɥit ʒə pãːs/
    Seven or eight I believe.

Pardon?
/pardɔ̃/
> *What?*

Ah oui, 40½ ou 42.
/ɑ wi karɑ̃t e dmi u karɑ̃t dø/
> *Oh yes, 40½ or 42.*

Les désirez-vous en noir/ brun/beige/blanc?
/le dezire vu ɑ̃ nwaːr brœ̃ bɛːʒ blɑ̃/
> *Would you like them in black/brown/beige/white?*

En noir.
/ɑ̃ nwaːr/
> *Black.*

Voici une paire 42.
/vwasi yn pɛr karɑ̃t dø/
> *Here's a 42.*

Merci. Celles-ci sont trop étroites/larges/grandes/petites.
/mɛrsi sɛl si sɔ̃ trop etrwat larʒ grɑ̃d pətit/
> *Thank you. These are too narrow/large/big/small.*

Pouvez-vous me donner un chausse-pied?
/puve vu m(ə) dɔne œ̃ ʃos pje/
> *Could you give me a shoehorn?*

Ça va, monsieur?
/sa va məsjø/
> *How's that, sir?*

Cela va très bien. Je prendrai aussi du cirage, une brosse et
/sla va trɛ bjɛ̃ ʒə prɑ̃dre osi dy siraːʒ yn brɔs e
une paire de chaussettes.
yn/ pɛr də ʃosɛt/
> *That's fine. I'll take some polish, a brush, and a pair of
> socks, too.*

Chez le disquaire

At the Record Store

REMARQUES

Certain stores specialize in records. There you can find the latest records and albums of French and international singing stars. You can also find records in large department stores.

Bonjour mademoiselle. Avez-vous des disques de Charles
/bɔ̃ʒuːr madəmwazɛl ave vu de disk də ʃarl
Aznavour?
aznavuːr/

    Good morning. Do you have any Charles Aznavour records?

Oui, madame.
/wi   madam/

    Yes ma'am.

J'aimerais son dernier album.
/ʒəmrɛ   sɔ̃ dɛrnje albɔm/

    I'd like his latest album.

Le voici, madame.
/lə vwasi madam/

    Here it is.

Puis-je l'écouter?
/pɥi ʒ lekute/

    May I listen to it?

Très certainement. Veuillez vous rendre dans la cabine 4.
/trɛ sɛrtɛnmã   vœje   vu   rãːdr   dã   la kabin katr/
Of course. Would you mind going to booth number 4.

Ce disque me plaît; je le prendrai.
/sə disk   mə plɛ   ʒə l prãdre/
I like this record; I'll take it.

Bien, madame.
/bjẽ   madam/
Fine.

Je voudrais aussi une cassette et un nouveau saphir pour ma
/ʒə vudrɛ(z) osi   yn   kasɛt   e   œ̃ nuvo   safiːr   pur   ma
chaîne stéréo.
ʃɛn   stereo/
I'd also like a cassette tape and a new needle for my stereo.

■ **Aimez-vous la musique?**   *Do you like music?*

musique campagnarde /myzik kãpaɲard/   country music
musique classique /myzik klasik/   classical music
musique de chambre /myzik də ʃãːbr/   chamber music
musique folklorique /myzik foklɔrik/   folk music
jazz /ʒaz/*m.*   jazz
musique légère /myzik leʒɛːr/   light music
musique pop /myzik pɔp/   pop music
musique symphonique /myzik sɛ̃fɔnik/   orchestral music
négro spirituels /negro spirityɛl/*m.*   Negro spirituals
rock /rɔk/*m.*   rock music

■ **Quelques vedettes**   *Some singing stars*

Charles Aznavour   Michel Sardou
Gilbert Bécaud   Mireille Mathieu

Jacques Brel   Sheila
Georges Brassens   Stone
Barbara   Sylvie Vartan
Johnny Halliday   Charden

Articles de photographie

Photographic Supplies

Je voudrais acheter l'appareil de photo en vitrine.
/ʒə vudrɛ(z) aʃte   laparɛj   də fɔto   ɑ̃ vitrin/
I'd like to buy the camera in the window.

Bien, mademoiselle. Voulez-vous aussi des pellicules?
/bjɛ̃   madəmwazɛl   vule   vu(z) osi   de pɛlikyl/
Yes, miss. Would you like film too?

Oui, très rapide et à grain fin.
/wi trɛ rapid e a grɛ̃ fɛ̃/
Yes, very fast film with a fine grain.

Noir et blanc?
/nwaːr e blɑ̃/
Black and white?

Non, un négatif couleur et aussi des diapositives.
/nɔ̃   œ̃ negatif kulœːr e osi   de djapozitiv/
No, a color negative and some slides too.

Pour lumière du jour ou artificielle?
/pur lymjɛr   dy ʒuːr u   artifisjɛl/
Daylight type or artificial light type?

Du jour, et donnez-moi aussi des ampoules flash.
/dy ʒuːr e dɔne   mwa osi   dez ɑ̃pul   flaʃ/
Daylight, and give me some flash bulbs too.

Bien, mademoiselle.
/bjɛ̃   madəmwazɛl/
Fine miss.

Est-ce que vous avez développé mes pellicules?
/ɛ   s   kə   vuz‿ave   devlɔpe   me   pɛlikyl/
Have you developed my films?

Oui, mademoiselle.   Voici vos négatifs.   Et voilà les épreuves.
/wi   madəmwazɛl   vwasi vo   negatif   e   vwala lez‿eprœːv/
Yes, (Miss).   Here are your negatives.   And here are the proofs.

Comment?   Il   n'y en a que quatre sur six de réussi?
/kɔmã   i(l) njãn‿a   kə   katr   syr sis də reysi/
What?   Only four out of six turned out O.K.?

En effet.   Un des clichés est trop exposé et l'autre n'est pas au
/ãn‿efɛ   œ̃ de kliʃe   ɛ   trop‿ɛkspoze e loːtr   nɛ   paz‿o
point.
pwɛ̃/
Right.   One of the negatives is overexposed and the other isn't in focus.

J'ai pourtant un bon appareil et un objectif très fin.
/ʒe purtã   œ̃ bɔn‿aparɛːj   e œ̃n‿ɔbʒɛktif trɛ fɛ̃/
Still I've got a good camera and a very sharp lens.

Vous n'avez pas eu de chance, mademoiselle.   Cela peut
/vu   nave   paz‿y də ʃãːs   madəmwazɛl   sla   pøt‿
arriver à tout le   monde.
arive   a tu   l(ə) mɔ̃d/
You just weren't lucky.   That can happen to anyone.

Ah, voilà un cliché qui est très net.   Pouvez-vous en faire un
/a   vwala œ̃ kliʃe ki   ɛ   trɛ nɛt   puve   vu   ã fɛr   œ̃n‿

agrandissement?
agrãdismã/

>Oh, there's a negative that's very clear. Can you make an
>enlargement of it?

Mais certainement. Quelle dimension? Huit (centimètres) sur
/mɛ sɛrtɛnmã   kɛl   dimãsjõ   ɥi   sãtimɛtr   syr
dix?
dis/

>Certainly. What size? Eight (centimeters) by ten?

Bien. Et tirez-en deux épreuves, une sur papier glacé et l'autre
/bjɛ̃ e tirez_ã døz_ eprœːv   yn syr papje glase e loːtr
sur papier mat.
syr papje mat/

>O.K. And make two prints, one with a glossy finish and the
>other one dull.

REMARQUES

Note that **appareil de photo** (m.) = *camera*, whereas **caméra**
(f.) = *movie camera*.

Blanchisserie-Teinturerie

Dry Cleaners

REMARQUES

You may have your clothes cleaned and your laundry washed, or you may do it yourself at a *laundromat* (**laveries automatiques**).

Bonjour madame. Je voudrais faire laver/nettoyer/repasser ces
/bɔ̃ʒuːr   madam   ʒə vudrɛ   fɛr lave nɛtwaje rəpɑse   se

vêtements.
vɛtmɑ̃/

Hello. I'd like these clothes washed/cleaned/ironed.

Oui monsieur. Vous avez un pantalon, deux vestes, deux
/wi   məsjø   vuz‿ave   œ̃ pɑ̃talɔ̃   dø   vɛst   dø

chemises, une jupe et une robe.
ʃmiz   yn ʒyp e yn rɔb/

Yes, sir. You have one pair of trousers, two suit jackets, two shirts, one skirt and one dress.

Quand cela sera-t-il prêt? Il me le faut le plus vite possible.
/kɑ̃   sla sra t il prɛ   i(l) mə l fo   lə ply vit pɔsibl/

When will they be ready? I need them as soon as possible.

Jeudi après-midi. Il vous faudra garder ce ticket.
/ʒødi aprɛ midi i(l) vu   fodra   garde sə tikɛ/

Thursday afternoon. You've got to keep this slip.

Faites-vous aussi des réparations? J'ai un trou dans mon
/fɛt   vu   osi   de   reparasjɔ̃   ʒe   œ̃   tru   dɑ̃   mɔ̃
pantalon.
ˈpɑ̃talɔ̃/

> *Would you also do some mending. There's a hole in my
> trousers.*

Oui, on peut le stopper si vous voulez.
/wi   ɔ̃   pø   lə   stɔpe   si   vu   vule/

> *Yes, we can mend it if you want.*

Est-ce que mon linge est prêt?
/ɛs   kə   mɔ̃   lɛ̃:ʒ   e   prɛ/

> *Is my laundry ready?*

Oui et toutes les taches sont parties.
/wi   e   tut   le   taʃ   sɔ̃   parti/

> *Yes and all the stains are out.*

Chez le bijoutier

At the Jeweler's

Regardez donc ce collier de   perles!
/rəgarde   dɔ̃(k) sə kɔlje   d(ə) pɛrl/
    Just look at that pearl necklace!

Et ce bracelet, que c'est beau!
/e sə braslɛ   k(ə) s ɛ   bo/
    And how pretty that bracelet is!

Moi, je n'aime pas l'émeraude. Et vous?
/mwa ʒə n ɛm   pɑ l emroːd   e vu/
    I don't like the emerald. Do you?

Je préfère le rubis et le   diamant.
/ʒə prefɛːr lə rybi e l(ə) djamã/
    I prefer the ruby and the diamond.

Et cette bague, comment la trouvez-vous?
/e sɛt bag   kɔmã   la truve   vu/
    And how do you like that ring?

La bague en or avec les diamants?
/la bag   ãn‿ɔːr avɛk le djamã/
    The gold ring with the diamonds?

L'autre, en platine avec les saphirs.
/l oːtr   ã platin avɛk le safiːr/
    The other one, the platinum with sapphires.

Elle est ravissante, très distinguée.
/ɛl ɛ ravisɑ̃ːt   trɛ distɛ̃ge/
It's charming, very elegant.

Oui, mais ça doit coûter une fortune.
/wi mɛ sa dwa kute   yn fɔrtyn/
Yes, but it must cost a fortune.

Evidemment. Et ce   pendentif?
/evidamɑ̃   e s(ə) pɑ̃dɑ̃tif/
Of course. What about that pendant?

En argent avec une turquoise?
/ɑ̃n‿arʒɑ̃ avɛk yn tyrkwaːz/
The silver one with the turquoise?

Oui, je crois que je   vais l'acheter.
/wi ʒə krwɑ kə   ʒ(ə) vɛ l aʃte/
Yes, I think I'll buy it.

Moi, j'aime ces boutons de manchettes.
/mwa ʒ ɛm se butɔ̃   də mɑ̃ʃɛt/
I like those cufflinks.

Demandons le prix au bijoutier.
/d(ə)mɑ̃dɔ̃   lə pri o biʒutje/
Let's ask the jeweler the price.

■ **Dans le magasin**   *In the store*

Pouvez-vous me montrer cela?
/puve vu mə mɔ̃tre   sla/
Could I please see that?

Avez-vous quelque chose en or/argent/platine?
/ave vu kɛlkə   ʃoːz ɑ̃n‿ɔːr arʒɑ̃   platin/
Do you have something in gold/silver/platinum?

Combien de carats?
/kɔ̃bjɛ̃   t kara/
How many carats is this?

Avez-vous quelque chose de meilleur marché?
/ave vu   kɛlkə   ʃoz   də mɛjœr   marʃe/
Do you have something more reasonable?

Faites-vous la réparation des montres?
/fɛt   vu   la reparasjɔ̃   de mɔ̃:tr/
Do you repair watches?

REMARQUES

1. You will find a jewelry counter in all department stores, but for more elegant jewelry, go to a jeweler.

2. Other vocabulary: **une alliance** /aljã:s/ = **un anneau de mariage** /ano d(ə) marja:ʒ/, *wedding ring*; **la breloque** /brəlɔk/, *charm, trinket*; **le camée** /kame/, *cameo*; **le collier** /kɔlje/, *necklace*; **la montre-bracelet** /mɔ̃:trbraslɛ/, *wristwatch*; **la chaîne** /ʃɛ:n/ **de montre**, *watch chain*; **le pendant d'oreille** /pãdã dɔrɛ:j/, *earring*; **le médaillon** /medajɔ̃/, *medallion*; **la médaille** /meda:j/, *medal*.

Le fleuriste

The Florist

Je voudrais un bouquet de fleurs.
/ʒə vudrɛ(z)   œ̃ bukɛ   d flœ̃ːr/
I'd like some flowers.

Bien monsieur.   Que désirez-vous?
/bjɛ̃ məsjø   kə dezire vu/
Fine sir.   What would you like?

Avez-vous des boutons de roses?
/ave vu   de butɔ̃   d roːz/
Do you have rosebuds?

J'ai des roses roses et des roses rouges.
/ʒe de roːz roːz e de roːz ruːʒ/
I have pink roses and red roses.

Je préfère les rouges.
/ʒə prefɛːr le ruːʒ/
I prefer the red ones.

Combien en voulez-vous?
/kɔ̃bjɛn   ɑ̃ vule   vu/
How many would you like?

Je ne sais pas, mais je voudrais que cela soit beau.
/ʒə n sɛ pɑ mɛ ʒə vudrɛ   kə sla swa bo/
I don't know, but I'd like it to be a nice bunch.

Alors neuf ou onze.
/alɔːr nœf u ɔ̃ːz/
> *Well then, nine or eleven.*

Quel est le prix, s'il vous plaît?
/kɛl ɛ lə pri si(l) vu plɛ/
> *What's the price please?*

C'est six francs la rose.
/sɛ si frã la roːz/
> *They're six francs a rose.*

C'est un peu cher.
/sɛt‿œ̃ pø ʃɛːr/
> *It's a little expensive.*

Voulez-vous des œillets, ils sont moins chers.
/vule vu dez‿œjɛ il sɔ̃ mwɛ̃ ʃɛːr/
> *Would you like carnations; they're less expensive.*

Oui, mais ils sont fanés. Donnez-moi neuf roses.
/wi mɛ il sɔ̃ fane dɔne mwa nœf roːz/
> *Yes, but they're faded. Give me nine roses.*

Bien monsieur.
/bjɛ̃ məsjø/
> *Yes sir.*

Je voudrais les faire livrer ce soir à huit heures.
/ʒə vudrɛ le fɛr livre sə swaːr a ɥit‿œːr/
> *I'd like to have them delivered this evening at eight.*

Voulez-vous écrire une petite carte?
/vule vuz‿ ekriːr yn ptit kart/
> *Would you like to write a card?*

Oui, s'il vous plaît.
/wi si(l) vu   plɛ/
> Yes, please.

Voici.
/vwasi/
> Here you are.

REMARQUES

1. In France you always give an uneven number of flowers. Ask the florist for advice.

2. Some flowers: **le muguet**/ lə mygɛ/, *lily of the valley*; **le lilas** /lə lila/, *lilac*; **la capucine** /kapysin/, *nasturtium*; **le myosotis** /mjɔzɔtis/, *forget-me-not*; **une orchidée** /ɔrkide/, *orchid*; **la violette** /vjɔlɛt/, *violet*; **le camélia** /kamelja/, *camelia*; **le réséda** /rezeda/, *mignonette*; **le lis** /lis/, *lily*; **la giroflée** /ʒirɔfle/, *stock*.

3. Additional vocabulary: **la gerbe**/ ʒɛːrb/, *bunch*; **le pot** /po/ **de fleurs**, *potted flowers*; **le pot à fleurs**, *flowerpot*.

Le kiosque à journaux

The Newsstand

Je   voudrais acheter un journal.
/ʒ(ə) vudrɛ(z) aʃte   œ̃ ʒurnal/
    I'd like to buy a newspaper.

Voilà justement un kiosque.
/vwala ʒystəmɑ̃   œ̃ kjɔsk/
    There's a paper stand right there.

(A la marchande) Le New York *Times*?
/a la marʃɑ̃ːd   lə   /
    (*To the vendor*) *The New York* Times?

Ah, monsieur, il   n'en reste plus.
/ɑ   məsjø   i(l) n ɑ̃ rɛst ply/
    I haven't got any left, sir.

Quel journal du matin vous reste-t-il?
/kɛl ʒurnal dy matɛ̃ vu   rɛst t i(l)/
    What morning paper do you have left?

Le Figaro, L'Humanité, L'Aurore.
/lə figaro l ymanite   lorɔːr/
    Le Figaro, L'Humanité, L'Aurore.

Le Figaro. Voici cinq francs.
/lə figaro vwasi sɛ̃   frɑ̃/
    Le Figaro. *Here are five francs.*

Voilà votre monnaie.
/vwala vɔt(r) mɔnɛ/
Here's your change.

Ah! j'oubliais — avez-vous un magazine des spectacles?
/a ʒublijɛ   ave vu   œ̃ magazin de spɛktakl/
Oh! I forgot — do you have a magazine for shows?

Oui! *Pariscope* ou l'Officiel des spectacles.
/wi   pariskɔp u l ɔfisjɛl de spɛktakl/
Yes! Pariscope *or the Officiel des spectacles.*

L'horaire des cinémas et des théâtres y est indiqué?
/l ɔrɛːr   de sinema e de teatr   i ɛt‿ ɛ̃dike/
*Are the times (lit. " schedule ") for movies and theaters
(indicated) in it?*

Oui, vous avez aussi les restaurants, les musées et les
/wi   vuz‿ave   osi   le rɛstɔrɑ̃   le myze e le
promenades.
prɔmnad/
*Yes, and you get restaurants, museums, and walks to take
too.*

Très bien. Donnez-moi *Pariscope*.
/trɛ bjɛ̃   dɔne   mwa pariskɔp/
O.K. Give me Pariscope *please.*

Voilà monsieur.
/vwala məsjø/
Here you are sir.

REMARQUES

Some additional vocabulary: **un abonnement** /abɔnmɑ̃/,
subscription; **un abonné** /abɔne/, *subscriber, holder of a season ticket*;
la manchette /mɑ̃ʃɛt/, *headline*; **une revue** /rəvy/, *magazine*; **une
publicité** /yn pyblisite/, *advertisement*; **faire de la publicité** /fer də
la pyblisite/, *to advertise*; **interviewer** /ɛ̃tɛrvjue/, *to interview.*

Chez le libraire

At the Bookstore

Madame pouvez-vous me renseigner?
/madam puve   vu   m(ə) rɑ̃sɛɲe/
  Could you help me?

Que puis-je faire pour vous?
/kə pɥi ʒ fɛːr pur vu/
  What can I do for you?

Je cherche un livre que je pourrais offrir à une jeune fille de
/ʒə ʃɛrʃ   œ̃ livr kə ʒ(ə) purɛ(z)͜ ɔfriːr a yn ʒœn fiːj də
quatorze ans.
katɔrz   ɑ̃/
  *I'm looking for a book that I can give to a fourteen-year-old
  girl.*

Oui, vous avez le rayon jeune au fond du magasin.
/wi vuz͜ave lə rɛjɔ̃ ʒœn o fɔ̃   dy magazɛ̃/
  *Yes, you'll find the section for young people at the back of
  the store.*

Avez-vous des livres de Balzac?
/ave vu de livr də balzak/
  Do you have books by Balzac?

Bien sûr, dans quelle collection?
/bjɛ̃ˑ syːr dɑ̃ kɛl   kɔlɛksjɔ̃/
  Of course; which series?

Je ne sais pas.
/ʒə n sɛ pɑ/
I don't know.

Nous avons des livres de luxe avec des illustrations.
/nuz‿avɔ̃ de livr də lyks avɛk dez‿ilystrɑsjɔ̃/
We have lovely illustrated hard-covered books.

Avez-vous quelque chose de moins cher?
/ave vu kɛlkə ʃoz də mwɛ̃ ʃɛːr/
Do you have something less expensive?

Oui, nous avons la collection Livres de poche, mais la
/wi nuz‿avɔ̃ la kɔlɛksjɔ̃ livr də pɔʃ mɛ la
couverture n'est pas cartonnée.
kuvɛrtyːr nɛ pɑ kartɔne/
*Yes, we have the Livres de poche series, but they're paper-
backs.*

Avez-vous des livres américains traduits en français?
/ave vu de livrəz‿amerikɛ̃ tradɥi ɑ̃ frɑ̃sɛ/
Do you have American books translated into French?

Certainement, les grands classiques et aussi les livres plus
/sɛrtɛnmɑ̃ le grɑ̃ klasik e osi le livr ply
récents.
resɑ̃/
Oh yes; the great classics and also more recent books.

Je voudrais le dernier livre qui a obtenu le Prix fémina.
/ʒə vudrɛ lə dɛrnje livr ki a ɔbtəny lə pri femina/
I'd like the last book that received the Prix fémina.

Très bien, madame.
/trɛ bjɛ̃   madam/
Fine.

REMARQUES

There is a difference between *bookstores* that sell new or used books and the **bouquinistes** who sell only old books, some of which have value.

Au bureau de tabac

At the Tobacco Shop

REMARQUES

Most tobacco shops are located in cafés and can be found by looking for a red sign reading "Tabac" outside the café. There are also independent stores that sell tobacco and smoking articles.

Donnez-moi un paquet de Winston et des allumettes.
/dɔne   mwa œ̃ pakɛ   d winstɔn e dez alymɛt/
Give me a pack of Winstons and some matches.

Vous désirez une boîte ou une pochette?
/vu   dezire yn bwat u yn pɔʃɛt/
Would you like a box or a book?

Donnez-moi une pochette; cela prend moins de place.
/dɔne   mwa yn pɔʃet   sla prɑ̃   mwɛ̃ də plas/
Give me a book; it takes up less room.

Voilà monsieur.
/vwala məsjø/
Here you are sir.

Avez-vous une recharge de gaz pour mon briquet?
/ave vu   yn rəʃarʒ   də gɑz pur mɔ̃ brikɛ/
Do you have a gas refill for my lighter?

Quelle est la marque?
/kɛl   ɛ la mark/
What brand is it?

C'est un Dupont. Je crois qu'il faut aussi changer la pierre.
/sɛt‿œ̃   dypɔ̃   ʒə krwa kil   fot‿ osi   ʃɑ̃ʒe   la pjɛːr/
It's a Dupont. I think the flint needs to be changed.

Oui, c'est exact mais je n'ai pas de pierre de rechange en ce
/wi   sɛt‿ɛgzakt   mɛ   ʒ(ə) ne pɑ t   pjɛːr   də r(ə)ʃarʒ   ɑ̃   sə
moment.
mɔmɑ̃/
Yes, that's right, but I don't have any flints right now.

Avez-vous des cigarettes françaises avec filtre?
/ave vu   de sigarɛt   frɑ̃sɛz   avɛk filtr/
Do you have French filter cigarettes?

Oui, des Gauloises ou des Gitanes.
/wi   de golwaːz   u de ʒitan/
Yes, Gauloises or Gitanes.

Donnez-moi deux paquets de Gitanes.
/dɔne   mwa dø   pakɛ   d ʒitan/
Give me two packs of Gitanes.

Chez le coiffeur (hommes)

At the Barber's

Pouvez-vous me couper les cheveux assez vite; j'ai rendez-vous
/puve vu m(ə) kupe le ʃvø   ase vit ʒe rɑ̃de vu
dans une demi-heure.
dɑ̃z yn dəmi œːr/
> *Could you give me a quick cut; I have an appointment in
> half an hour.*

Oui, monsieur; une coupe au rasoir ou aux ciseaux?
/wi məsjø   yn kup o rɑzwaːr u o   sizo/
> *Yes sir; a razor cut or a scissor cut?*

Au rasoir, mais pas trop court; c'est juste pour rafraîchir.
/o rɑzwaːr mɛ pɑ tro kuːr sɛ ʒyst pur rafrɛʃir/
> *A razor cut, but not too short; just a trim.*

Coupez encore un peu en arrière/sur les côtés/dans la nuque.
/kupe ɑ̃kɔːr œ̃ pø ɑ̃n‿arjɛːr syr le kote dɑ̃ la nyk/
> *Cut a little more in the back/on the sides/in the neck.*

Je vous fais une friction?
/ʒə vu fɛ yn friksjɔ̃/
> *Should I give you a scalp massage?*

Non merci.
/nɔ̃ mɛrsi/
> *No, thank you.*

Bien monsieur, désirez-vous être rasé?
/bjɛ̃ məsjø   dezire vu   ɛtr(ə) raze/
Very well, sir; would you like a shave?

Oui, mais seulement la barbe; ne touchez ni la moustache ni
/wi mɛ sœlmã   la barb   nə tuʃe   ni la mustaʃ   ni
les favoris.
le favɔri/
*Yes, but just a regular shave; don't touch my mustache
or my sideburns.*

Désirez-vous de la brillantine?
/dezire vu   d la brijãtin/
Would you like hair tonic?

Ah! Non, surtout pas.
/a   nɔ̃   syrtu   pa/
Oh! No (lit. " especially not ")!

REMARQUES

An appointment is not necessary at the barber's.

Chez le coiffeur (femmes)

At the Hairdresser's

Y a-t-il un salon de coiffure à l'hôtel?
/j a t il œ̃ salɔ̃ də kwafyːr a l otɛl/
   Is there a beauty parlor in the hotel?

Non, madame. Il y en a un au coin de la rue. Il faut prendre
/nɔ̃   madam   i(l) i ɑ̃n a œ̃ o kwɛ̃ d la ry   i(l) fo prɑ̃ːdr
rendez-vous.
rɑ̃de   vu/
   *No, ma'am. There's one at the corner of the street. You
   have to make an appointment.*

Je voudrais... /ʒə vudrɛ/		*I would like . . .*
un shampooing /œ̃ ʃapwɛ̃/		*a shampoo*
une coloration /yn kɔlɔrasjɔ̃/		*a(n)*
châtain roux /ʃatɛ̃ ru/		*auburn*
blonde /blɔ̃d/		*blond*
brune /bryn/		*brown hair color*
une décoloration		*a bleach*
/yn dekɔlɔrasjɔ̃/		
une mise en plis /yn miz ɑ̃ pli/		*a set*
une permanente /yn pɛrmanɑ̃ːt/		*a permanent*
une teinture /yn tɛtyːr/		*my hair dyed*
une coupe /yn kup/		*a haircut*
un chignon /œ̃ ʃiɲɔ̃/		*a chignon, a bun*
un masque de beauté		*a face mask*
/œ̃ mask də bote/		
une manucure /yn manykyːr/		*a manicure*

une pédicure   /yn pediky:r/   *a pedicure*
une épilation   /yn epilɑsjɔ̃/   *an epilatory treatment*
un nouveau maquillage   *new make-up*
   /œ̃ nuvo makija:ʒ/
      pour les lèvres   /pur le lɛ:vr/   *for my lips*
      pour les yeux   /pur lez‿jø/   *for my eyes*
      pour les joues   /pur le ʒu/   *for my cheeks*

J'ai les cheveux   /ʒe le ʃvø/   *My hair is*
   raides   /rɛd/   *straight*
   bouclés   /bukle/   *curly*
   ondulés   /ɔ̃dyle/   *wavy*

Puis-je avoir   une permanente?
/pɥi ʒ avwa:r yn pɛrmanɑ̃:t/
      May I have a permanent?

Certainement madame.
/sɛrtɛnmɑ̃   madam/
      Certainly, madame.

Mes cheveux sont horribles.
/me ʃvø   sɔ̃t‿ɔribl/
      My hair is terrible.

Oh, non, madame, mais   un peu huileux.
/o nɔ̃ madam mɛ(z)‿œ̃ pø ɥilø/
      Oh, no, madam, but it's a little oily.

Il   faudrait un bon shampooing?
/i(l) fodrɛ   œ̃ bɔ̃ ʃɑ̃pwɛ̃/
      Does it need a good shampoo?

Ah, oui! Quelle coiffure désirez-vous?
/ɑ wi kɛl   kwafy:r dezire vu/
      Oh, yes! What style do you prefer?

Lissez-moi les cheveux en arrière.
/lise mwa le ʃvø   ɑ̃‿arjɛːr/
Smooth the hair straight back.

Je   vais les friser sur le front?
/ʒ(ə) vɛ le frize syr lə frɔ̃/
Shall I curl it on the forehead?

Non. Sur les tempes et la nuque.
/nɔ̃   syr le tɑ̃ːp   e la nyk/
No. Over the temples and in the back (of the neck).

Cette coiffure vous va très bien.
/sɛt   kwafyːr vu   va trɛ bjɛ̃/
This style is very becoming to you.

Vous trouvez? Ça fait assez jeune?
/vu   truve   sa fɛ ase ʒœn/
You think so? Does it make me look younger?

Ça fait très jeune fille.
/sa fɛ trɛ ʒœn fiːj/
It makes you look like a young girl.

Faites-moi aussi un traitement de la peau.
/fɛt   mwa osi œ̃ trɛtmɑ̃   d la po/
Give me a facial too.

Bien, madame. Comme vous voudrez.
/bjɛ̃   madam   kɔm   vu   vudre/
Very well, madam. As you wish.

Attention! Vous me brûlez!
/atɑ̃sjɔ̃   vu   m(ə) bryle/
Be careful! You're burning me!

Oh, pardon! L'eau est très chaude.
/o pardɔ̃ l o ɛ trɛ ʃoːd/
Oh, excuse me. The water's very hot.

A la pharmacie

At the Drugstore

A quelle heure ouvre/ferme la pharmacie?
/a kɛl   œːr   uvr   /fɛrm   la farmasi/
What time does the drugstore open/close?

Où est la pharmacie de garde?
/u   ɛ   la farmasi   d gard/
Where's the all-night drugstore?

Bonjour, monsieur. Vous désirez?
/bɔ̃ʒuːr   məsjø   vu   dezire/
Good afternoon, sir. What would you like?

J'ai une ordonnance du médecin.
/ʒ e yn   ɔrdɔnãːs   dy medsɛ̃/
I have a doctor's prescription.

Bien. On va vous la préparer.
/bjɛ̃   ɔ̃   va vu   la prepare/
All right. We'll fill it for you.

Et un flacon de teinture d'iode.
/e œ̃ flakɔ̃ d(ə) tɛ̃tyːr   d jɔd/
And a small bottle of tincture of iodine.

Oui, monsieur. Et avec cela?
/wi   məsjø   e avɛk sla/
Yes, sir. Anything else (lit. " and with that ")?

Oh, quelque chose pour la toux.
/o kɛlk   ʃoːz pur la tu/
Oh, something for a cough.

Ces pastilles sont très efficaces.
/se pastiːj sɔ̃   trɛz ɛfikas/
These cough drops are very effective.

Bien. Je   crois que c'est tout.
/bjɛ̃   ʒ(ə) krwɑ k(ə) s ɛ tu/
All right. I think that's all.

Voilà. Tout est dans ce paquet.
/vwala tut ɛ   dɑ̃   sə pakɛ/
There you are. Everything's in this package.

Merci bien. Au revoir,   monsieur.
/mɛrsi bjɛ̃   ɔ   r(ə)vwaːr məsjø/
Thank you. Good-bye.

REMARQUES

1. Drugstores in France sell only medicine and health-related products such as baby food, exercise equipment, etc. You may also obtain the following: **bandes** (f.) /bɑ̃d/, *bandages*; **compresses** (f.) /kɔ̃prɛs/, *sterile pads*; **la teinture d'iode** /tɛtyːr djɔd/, *iodine*; **le mercurochrome** /mɛrkyrɔkrom/, *mercurochrome*; **vitamines** (f.) /vitamin/, *vitamins/*; **désinfectants** (m.) /dezɛ̃fɛktɑ̃/, *disinfectants*. For more sophisticated medicine, a doctor's prescription is required.

2.   If you have a cold or flu: **Je voudrais quelque chose contre la grippe /un rhume** /ʒə vudrɛ kɛlkə ʃoːz kɔ̃tr la grip œ̃ rym/, *I'd like something for flu /a cold.* Other vocabulary: **une aspirine** /aspirin/, *aspirin*; **le sirop contre la toux** /siro kɔ̃tr la tu/, *cough syrup*; **des gouttes** (f.) **pour le nez** /gut pur lə ne/, *nose drops*; **des pastilles** (f.) **pour la gorge/** de pastiːj pur la gɔrʒ/, *throat lozenges*.

3. Some additional useful words: **le pharmacien**/farmasjɛ̃/, *pharmacist*; **la quinine** /kinin/, *quinine*; **le thermomètre** /tɛrmɔmɛtr/, *thermometer*; **la blessure** /blɛsyːr/, *wound*; **le bicarbonate** /bikarbɔnat/, *bicarbonate*; **un rhume de cerveau** /rym də sɛrvo/, *head cold*; **rhume de poitrine** /pwatrin/, *chest cold*; **être enrhumé** /ɑ̃ryme/, *to have a cold*; **souffrir de l'estomac** /sufrir d(ə) lɛstoma/, *to have stomach trouble*.

Le médecin

The Doctor

■ **Si vous avez un accident**   *If you have an accident*

Y a-t-il un médecin ici?
/j a t il œ̃ medsɛ̃   isi/
   Is there a doctor here?

Non, je ne crois pas.
/nɔ̃   ʒə n   krwa pɑ/
   No, I don't think so.

Alors, téléphonez immédiatement à un médecin/une ambulance/
/alɔːr telefɔne   immedjatmɑ̃   a œ̃ medsɛ̃   yn ɑ̃bylɑ̃ːs
police-secours.
pɔlis   səkuːr/
   Then call a doctor/an ambulance/emergency right away.

Madame je suis médecin. Où avez-vous mal?
/madam ʒə sɥi medsɛ̃   u ave vu   mal/
   I'm a doctor. Where does it hurt?

J'ai mal à la tête/au bras/au dos/à la jambe/au ventre/à
/ʒe   mal a la tɛt o   bra o   do a la ʒɑ̃b   o   vɑ̃ːtr   a
l'épaule.
lepol/
   My head/arm/back/leg/stomach/shoulder hurts.

Allongez-vous et ne bougez pas.
/alɔ̃ʒe vu e nə buʒe   pɑ/
   Lie down and don't move.

J'ai une douleur ici.
/ʒe yn dulœːr isi/
I have a pain here.

Respirez profondément.
/rɛspire prɔfɔ̃demɑ̃/
Breathe deeply.

Cela me fait mal.
/sla mə fɛ mal/
That hurts me.

Je vais vous faire une piqûre.
/ʒə vɛ vu fɛr yn pikyːr/
I'm going to give you an injection.

Docteur, est-ce grave?
/dɔktœːr ɛ s grav/
Doctor, is it serious?

Non, ne vous inquiétez pas.
/nɔ̃ nə vuz‿ɛ̃kjete pɑ/
No, don't worry.

Dois-je aller à l'hôpital?
/dwa ʒ ale a l ɔpital/
Do I have to go to the hospital?

Oui, mais seulement en observation.
/wi mɛ sœlmɑ̃ ɑ̃n‿ɔbzɛrvasjɔ̃/
Yes, but only for observation.

■ **Si vous vous sentez mal**   *If you don't feel well*

Y a-t-il un médecin qui parle anglais?
/j a t il œ̃ medsɛ̃ ki parl ɑ̃glɛ/
Is there a doctor here who speaks English?

Non, madame.
/nɔ̃   madam/
No ma'am.

Est-ce que le   médecin peut venir à domicile?
/ɛ s kə l(ə) medsɛ̃   pø vnir a dɔmisil/
Does the doctor make house calls?

Oui, mais il vous faudra attendre.
/wi mɛ(z) il vu   fodra atɑ̃ːdr/
Yes, but you will have to wait.

A quelle heure peut-il venir?
/a kɛl   œːr   pøt il vənir/
What time can he come?

Dans l'après-midi.
/dɑ̃ l aprɛ midi/
In the afternoon.

Docteur, je suis malade.
/dɔktœːr ʒə sɥi malad/
Doctor, I'm sick.

Qu'est-ce qui ne va pas?
/k ɛ s ki n(ə) va pɑ/
What's the trouble?

J'ai mal partout et je me sens faible.
/ʒe mal partu   e ʒə m sɑ̃   fɛbl/
I ache all over and I feel weak.

Depuis combien de temps avez-vous mal?
/dəpɥi kɔ̃bjɛ̃   t tɑ̃   ave vu mal/
How long have you been ill?

Depuis deux jours.
/dəpyi dø ʒuːr/
Two days.

Etes-vous constipée?
/ɛt vu kɔ̃stipe/
Are you constipated?

Non, au contraire j'ai la diarrhée et des nausées.
/nɔ̃ o kɔ̃trɛːr ʒe la djare e de noze/
No, quite the reverse; I have diarrhea and nausea.

Avez-vous des vomissements?
/ave vu de vɔmismã/
Are you vomiting?

Oui en me réveillant.
/wi ã mə revɛjã/
Yes when I wake up.

Qu'avez-vous mangé hier?
/k ave vu mãʒe jɛːr/
What did you eat yesterday?

Du pâté et de la viande en sauce.
/dy pɑte e d la vjãːd ã sos/
Pâté and some meat and gravy.

Bon, je vais vous donner une ordonnance et des médicaments.
/bɔ̃ ʒə vɛ vu dɔne yn ɔrdɔnãːs e de medikamã/
Well then, I'll give you a prescription and medication.

Docteur, qu'est-ce que j'ai?
/dɔktœːr k ɛ s kə ʒe/
Doctor, what do I have?

Oh! une petite intoxication alimentaire.
/o   yn ptit   ɛ̃tɔksikɑsjɔ̃ alimɑ̃tɛːr/
Oh! slight food poisoning.

Dois-je rester coucher?
/dwa ʒ rɛste kuʃe/
Do I have to stay in bed?

Oui, pendant deux ou trois jours, et vous prendrez deux pilules
/wi pɑ̃dɑ̃   dø u trwa ʒuːr e vu prɑ̃dre dø pilyl
deux fois par jour avant chaque repas/après les repas/matin et
dø   fwa par ʒuːr avɑ̃   ʃak   rəpɑ aprɛ le rəpɑ matɛ̃ e
soir.
swaːr/

       Yes, for two or three days, and take two pills twice a day
       before each meal/after meals/morning and night.

Merci, docteur. Combien vous dois-je?
mɛrsi dɔktœːr kɔ̃bjɛ̃   vu   dwa ʒ/
       Thank you Doctor. How much do I owe you?

Cent francs. Au revoir   madame.
/sɑ̃   frɑ̃   ɔ r(ə)vwaːr madam/
       A hundred francs. Good-bye.

Chez le dentiste

At the Dentist's

Vous avez mal aux dents? Laquelle vous fait mal?
/vuz‿ave mal o dã   lakɛl   vu fɛ mal/
Do you have a toothache? Which one hurts?

Celle-ci, cette molaire dans la mâchoire supérieure, à gauche.
/sɛl si sɛt mɔlɛːr dã la maʃwaːr syperjœːr a goʃ/
This one, this molar in the upper jaw, on the left.

Depuis quand vous fait-elle mal?
/dəpɥi kã   vu fɛt ɛl mal/
How long has it been giving you trouble?

Depuis plusieurs jours, mais je ne souffrais pas beaucoup.
/dəpɥi plyzjœr ʒuːr mɛ ʒə n sufrɛ   pɑ boku/
*Several days, but it wasn't really painful (lit. " I wasn't
suffering much ").*

Et maintenant, vous souffrez davantage?
/e mɛ̃tnã   vu   sufre   davãtaːʒ/
And now it's more painful?

J'ai un mal terrible. Je n'ai pas dormi de la nuit.
/ʒə œ̃ mal tɛribl   ʒə ne   pɑ dɔrmi d(ə) la nɥi/
I have a terrible pain. I didn't sleep all night.

Cette dent est cariée. Vouz avez peut-être un abcès.
/sɛt dã ɛ karje vuz‿ave   pøt ɛtr œ̃n‿apsɛ/
That tooth is decayed. You probably have an abscess.

Aïe! vous me faites mal, docteur. Vous avez touché le nerf.
/aj vu   mə fɛt   mal dɔktœːr vuz‿ave   tuʃe   l(ə) nɛːr/
Oh! You're hurting me, Doctor. You hit the nerve.

Je pourrai peut-être la sauver. Mais il faut faire une radio.
/ʒe pure   pøt ɛtr   la sove   mɛ(z) il fo   fɛr   yn radjo/
*Perhaps I'll be able to save it. But we'll have to take an
x-ray first.*

Vous croyez qu'il ne sera pas nécessaire de l'arracher?
/vu   krwaje kil   nə sra pɑ nesesɛːr   də laraʃe/
You don't think I'll have to have it out?

J'espère que non. On verra.
/ʒɛspɛːr k(ə) nɔ̃   ɔ̃ vɛra/
I hope not. We'll see.

Alors, il suffira de la plomber, n'est-ce pas?
/alɔːr il syfira d la plɔ̃be   nɛs   pɑ/
*In that case, a filling will do, won't it (lit. " it will suffice to
fill it ")?*

Oui. Revenez me voir   demain, à la même heure.
/wi   rəvne   mə vwaːr dəmɛ̃   a la mɛm   œːr/
Yes. Come back and see me tomorrow, at the same time.

Mais en attendant j'aurai toujours mal?
/mɛ(z) ɑ̃n‿atɑ̃dɑ̃   ʒɔre   tuʒuːr   mal/
But meanwhile will it still hurt me?

Mais non. Ce médicament vous empêchera de souffrir.
/mɛ   nɔ̃   sə medikamɑ̃   vuz‿ɑ̃pɛʃra   d sufrir/
Oh, no. This medicine will stop the pain.

REMARQUES

  1. Some useful expressions: **le cabinet du dentiste** /kabinɛ dy
dɑ̃tist/, *dentist's office*; **heures (f.) de consultation** /œːr də kɔ̃syltɑsjɔ̃/,

office hours; **à quelle heure pourriez-vous me donner une consultation?**
a kɛl œːr purje vu mdɔne yn kɔ̃syltɑsjɔ̃/, *what time could you give
me an appointment for?*

2. Some words suggested by the text: **la radiographie**
/radjografi/, *X-ray*; **le plombage** /plɔ̃baːj/, *filling*; **anesthésier**
/anɛstezje/, *to anesthetize*; **gencives** (f.) /ʒɑ̃siv/, *gums*; **fausses dents**
/fos dɑ̃/, *false teeth.*

Au secours

Help in Paris

Useful telephone numbers

Police gendarmerie: 17.	police
Pompiers, ambulances: 18.	fire, ambulance
Télégrammes: 14.	telegrams
Renseignements: 12.	information

- **Trains autos-couchettes**   *Sleepers*

Lyon	(de 7 h à 20 h)	307-71-19
Austerlitz	(de 7 h à 20 h)	584-43-65
Wagons-lits		073-61-30

- **R.A.T.P.**   *Subway and buses*
Le plus court chemin d'un point à un autre en région
parisienne (24 h sur 24) 346-14-14

- **Radio-taxis**   *Taxis*

252-94-00 735-22-22 657-11-12
739-33-33 205-77-77
203-99-99 200-67 89

- **Location de voitures sans chauffeur**   *Car rentals*
(du lundi au vendredi de 8 h 30 à 19 h, le samedi de
8 h 30 à 18 h) 292-02-92

- **Télévision**   *Television*
Programmes   INF 2 555-92-22

- **Transport de marchandises**   *Freight*

Allô Fret	655-88-80
G 7 Fret	739-33-44
S.V.P. Transport Rive Droite	270-15-15
S.V.P. Transport Rive Gauche	326-97-00
S.V.P. Transport Nation	371-88-88

- **Etat des routes**   *Road conditions*
  704-60-30 858-33-33
- **Objets perdus**   *Lost and found*
  531-82-10
- **E.D.F. - G.D.F.**   *Electricity and Gas*
  Urgences E.D.F. 522-90-00
  Urgences G.D.F. 282-20-20
- **P.T.T.**   *Post office; Telegraph; Telephone*
  Renseignements jours ouvrables 280-67-89
  dim. et fêtes 508-01-33
  Bureau ouvert tous les jours sans exception et 24 h
  sur 24:
  Paris RP 52, rue du Louvre 508-01-35
  Chèques postaux................ 533-74-00
- **SOS Amitié**   *Hot line*
  (24h sur 24) 825-70-50
- **Garde d'enfants**   *Day care centers*
  Association des Etudiants en Médecine, 26, Fg-St-Jacques. Odé. 25-44. Bureau ouv. de 10 h à 19 h. Tarif 8 F l'heure plus déplacement. Après dernier métro, retour par voiture. Minimum de garde: 3 h A 12 h et 19 h 30 avec repas.

  Institut Catholique de Paris, 21, rue d'Assas. 548-31-70. Bureaux ouverts de 9 à 12 h et de 14 h à 18 h. Tarif: 9 F l'heure. 10 F après minuit.

  Comité parisien des œuvres des Etudiants, 39, av. de l'Observatoire. Dan. 07-49. Poste 437. Ouv. de 9 h à 17 h 30 (sauf samedi). Garde toute la journée jusqu'à 22 h: 9 F l'heure. Après 22 h: 10 F. Plus déplacement; minimum 3 h.

Services téléphoniques d'urgence. Appelez   *Emergencies*

- **Services médicaux**   *Medical*
  S.O.S. Médecin (24 h sur 24) 707-77-77
  S.O.S. Docteur nuit (24 h sur 24) 337-77-77
  S.O.S. Santé (8 h à 23 h)................ 655-25-35

S.A.M.U. (Service Aide Médicale d'Urgence)
(24 h sur 24) 567-50-50
A.U.M.P. (Association pour les Urgences Médicales
de Paris) (24 h sur 24) 578-61-38
Brûlures graves *Burns:*
    Hôpital Cochin 329-21-21
    Hôpital Foch.. 506-18-00
Centre anti-poison *Poison* 205-63-29
Transfusions sanguines 307-47-28

■ **Services pharmaceutiques** *Pharmaceutical*
Pharmacie ouverte toute la nuit :
    Pharmacie Proniewski, 5, place Blanche................ 874-77-99
Pharmacie ouverte jusqu'à 1 h du matin :
    Pharmacie des Arts, 106, bd Montparnasse 326-56-20
Pharmacie ouverte jusqu'à 24 h :
    Pharmacie Mozart, 14, av. Mozart.................. 527-38-17

■ **Services ambulanciers** *Ambulance*
Ambulances de l'Assistance Publique 887-27-50
Association Parisienne du Secours Ambulancier........ 535-18-66

■ **Services vétérinaires** *Veterinary*
S.O.S. Vétérinaire
    Paris (de 20 h à 8 h) et jours fériés 288-67-99
    Périphérie (vétérinaires de garde)................ 602-45-07

Renseignements généraux   *Information*

■ **Aéroports de Paris**
Renseignements et horaires :
    Orly .... 687-12-34 et 587-51-41
    Le Bourget.. 834-93-90
    Roissy.. 862-22-80

■ **Air France**
Renseignements et réservations 535-66-00
        535-61-61

■ **Air Inter**
Renseignements et réservations 539-25-25
Fret 687-12-12

- **U.T.A.**
  Renseignements 266-30-30
  Réservation 776-41-52

- **S.N.C.F.**   *Trains*
  Renseignements *Information*
  Bureau central (de 8 h à 22 h) 261-50-50
  Est   (de 6 h à 24 h) 208-49-90
  Nord   (de 6 h à 24 h) 526-77-28
  Saint-Lazare   (de 6 h à 24 h) 538-52-29
  Montparnasse   (de 6 h à 24 h) 538-52-29
  Austerlitz   (de 6 h à 24 h) 584-16-16
  Lyon   (de 6 h à 24 h) 345-92-22

  Enlèvement des bagages à domicile   *Pick-up*

  Bureau central (de 9 h à 12 h 30) ....
                  (de 14 h à 18 h) 261-50-50
  Est   (de 6 h à 24 h) 208-89-87
  Nord   (de 6 h à 24 h) 878-08-41
  Saint-Lazare   (de 6 h à 24 h) 522-74-30
  Montparnasse   (de 6 h à 24 h) 548-20-73
  Austerlitz   (de 6 h à 24 h) 584-43-53
  Lyon   (de 6 h à 24 h) 343-14-52

A la banque

At the Bank

Où est la banque la plus proche?
/u ε la bã:k   la ply prɔʃ/
Where is the nearest bank?

La B.N.P. se trouve sur le boulevard.
/la be ɛn pe sə truv   syr lə bulva:r/
There's a B.N.P. (National Bank of Paris) on the boulevard.

Je voudrais changer des dollars en francs.
/ʒə vudrɛ   ʃãʒe   de dɔla:r ã frã/
I'd like to change some dollars into francs.

Vous avez des travelers ou du liquide?
/vuz‿ave   de travlœrz u dy likid/
Do you have traveler's checks or cash?

Des travelers. Quel est le cours?
/de travlœrz kɛl ɛ l(ə) ku:r/
Traveler's. What's the rate of exchange?

Le dollar est à 4 francs 99 pour les travelers.
/lə dɔla:r ɛt‿ a katr frã katr vɛ̃ diz nœf pur le travlœrz/
The dollar is at 4 francs 99 for traveler's checks.

Merci. Je voudrais des billets de cent francs et de la petite
/mɛrsi ʒə vudrɛ   de bijɛ   d sã frã   e d la ptit
monnaie.
mɔnɛ/
Thank you. I'd like hundred-franc bills and some change.

Vous avez votre passeport?
/vuz‿ave   vɔtr paspɔːr/
  Do you have your passport?

Je   voudrais ouvrir un compte.
/ʒ(ə) vudrɛ(z) uvriːr œ̃ kɔ̃ːt/
  I'd like to open an account.

Je   voudrais déposer mille dollars.
/ʒ(ə) vudrɛ   depoze mil dɔlaːr/
  I'd like to deposit a thousand dollars.

Je   vous donnerai un livret de banque.
/ʒ(ə) vu   dɔnre   œ̃ livrɛ d(ə) bɑ̃ːk/
  I'll give you a passbook.

Et un carnet de chèques, s'il vous plaît.
/e œ̃ karnɛ d(ə) ʃɛk   s i(l) vu   plɛ/
  And a checkbook, please.

Certainement. En voici un.
/sɛrtɛnmɑ̃   ɑ̃   vwasi œ̃/
  Certainly. Here's one.

Cette banque a des succursales?
/sɛt bɑ̃ːk   a de sykyrsal/
  Has this bank any branches?

Dans toutes les grandes villes.
/dɑ̃ tut le grɑ̃ːd vil/
  In all the large cities.

C'est bien commode quand on voyage.
/s ɛ bjɛ̃ kɔmɔd   kɑ̃t‿ɔ̃   vwajaːʒ/
  That's very convenient when a person travels.

Surtout pour toucher vos chèques.
/syrtu   pur tuʃe   vo ʃɛk/
  Especially for cashing your checks.

Alors, je n'aurai pas de difficultés?
/alɔːr ʒ(ə) n ɔre   pɑ d difikylte/
Then I'll have no trouble?

Pas du tout, je vous assure.
/pɑ dy tu   ʒ(ə) vuz‿asyːr/
None at all, I assure you.

REMARQUES

1. Banks are generally open from 9 A.M. to 4 P.M., Monday through Friday. Traveler's checks are accepted almost everywhere, as well as certain credit cards.

The currency is francs and centimes (100 centimes = 1 franc). There are coins in the following denominations: 5, 10, 20, 50 (centimes); 1, 5, and 10 (francs). Notes come in denominations of: 10, 50, 100, 500 (francs).

The rate of exchange is published daily in the newspaper *Le Monde.*

2. Some additional words: **une action** /aksjɔ̃/, *share*; **le banquier** /bɑ̃kje/, *banker*; **le billet** /bijɛ/ **de banque**, *bank note*; **la bourse** /burs/, *stock exchange*; **un emprunt** /ɑ̃prœ̃/, *loan*; **emprunter** /ɑ̃prœ̃te/, *to loan*; **les frais** (m.) /frɛ/, *expenses*; **une obligation** ɔbligasjɔ̃/, *bond*; **prêter** /prɛte/, *to lend*; **pouvez-vous me prêter. . .?** /puve vu m(ə) prɛte/, *can you lend me . . .?* **la taxe, un impôt** /taks ɛ̃po/, *tax*; **le revenu** /rəvny/, *income.*

A la poste

At the Post Office

Où se trouve la poste la plus proche?
/u sə truv   la pɔst la ply prɔʃ/
Where's the nearest post office?

Où est le guichet des lettres pour l'étranger?
/u ɛ l(ə) giʃɛ   de lɛtr   pur l etrãʒe/
Where's the window for overseas mail?

Combien de timbres faut-il pour les Etats-Unis?
/kɔ̃bjɛ̃   t tɛbr   fot_il pur lez‿etaz‿yni/
What's the postage for the U.S.?

Où peut-on toucher un mandat international?
/u pøt‿ɔ̃ tuʃe   œ̃ mãda ɛ̃tɛrnasjɔnal/
Where can I cash an international money order?

Où est la poste restante?
/u ɛ la pɔst rɛstã:t/
Where's the general delivery window?

Avez-vous du courrier pour moi; je suis Mme. Smith.
/ave vu   dy kurje   pur mwa ʒə sɥi madam smit/
Do you have any mail for me; I am Mrs. Smith.

Je voudrais envoyer un colis.
/ʒə vudrɛ(z) ãvwaje œ̃ kɔli/
I'd like to send a package.

Où est la boîte aux lettres?
/u ɛ   la bwat o   lɛtr/
Where is the mail box?

REMARQUES

1.   You will find a post office in each district of the city. The telephone and telegraph service is located in the post office, hence the expression P.T.T. (**Poste, Télégraphe, Téléphone**). Hours are from 8:00 A.M. to 7:00 P.M., Monday through Friday, and 8:00 A.M. to noon on Saturdays.

2.   Some important expressions: **par avion** /par avjɔ̃/, *airmail*; **en express** /ãn‿ɛksprɛs/, *special delivery*; **en recommandé** /ã rəkɔmãde/, *registered mail.*

3.   Letters addressed "General Delivery (**Poste Restante**), Paris" without a specific post office may be picked up at the main post office: 52 rue du Louvre, 75001–Paris.

Télégramme et téléphone

Telegram and Telephone

Je voudrais envoyer un télégramme.
/ʒə vudrɛ(z) ɑ̃vwaje œ̃ telegram/
I'd like to send a telegram.

Oui madame. Remplissez ce formulaire.
/wi madam   rɑ̃plise   s(ə) fɔrmylɛːr/
Yes ma'am.   Fill in this form.

Combien coûte le mot?
/kɔ̃bjɛ̃   kut   lə mo/
What is the rate per word?

Quand arrivera-t-il à Chicago?
/kɑ̃   arivra   t il a ʃikago/
When will it arrive in Chicago?

Demain dans la journée, à cause du décalage horaire.
/dəmɛ̃   dɑ̃   la ʒurne   a koz   dy dekalaʒ   ɔrɛːr/
Tomorrow, during the day, because of the time change.

Très bien. Combien vous dois-je?
/trɛ bjɛ̃   kɔ̃bjɛ̃   vu   dwa ʒ/
Fine. How much do I owe you?

Trente francs.
/trɑ̃t   frɑ̃/
Thirty francs.

Voilà. Merci madame.
/vwala mɛrsi madam/
Here you are. Thank you ma'am.

Où est le   téléphone?
/u ɛ   l(ə) telefɔn/
Where's the telephone?

Vous avez une cabine téléphonique dans le métro.
/vuz‿ave   yn kabin telefɔnik   dã l(ə) metro/
There's a phone booth in the subway.

Avez-vous un annuaire, et pouvez-vous m'aider à obtenir ce
/ave vu   œ̃n‿anɥɛːr   e puve   vu   mɛde   a ɔbtənir sə
numéro?
nymero/
Do you have a phone book and could you help me get this number?

Bonjour. Je voudrais téléphoner à Lyon.
/bɔ̃ʒuːr ʒə vudrɛ   telefɔne   a ljɔ̃/
Hello. I'd like to call Lyon.

Quel numéro?
/kɛl nymero/
What number please?

J'aimerais téléphoner en préavis/en p.c.v.
/ʒɛmrɛ   telefɔne ã preavi /ã pe se ve/
I would like to call person to person/collect.

Le nom de la personne?
/lə nɔ̃   d la pɛrsɔn/
The name?

M.   Durand.
/məsjø dyrã/
Mr. Durand.

Ne quittez pas monsieur. . . (Dix minutes plus tard)
/nə kite   pɑ məsjø/
One moment please . . . (Ten minutes later)

■ **Il est là**   *He Is In*

Allez-y monsieur, vous avez la communication.
/alez‿ i məsjø   vuz‿ ave la kɔmynikɑsjɔ̃/
Go ahead sir, your call has gone through.

Allo, M.   Durand, ici c'est Mr.   Smith.
/alo məsjø dyrɑ̃   isi sɛ   məsjø smit/
Hello, M. Durand, this is Mr. Smith.

■ **Il n'est pas là**   *He Is Not In*

L'abonné ne répond pas.
/labɔne   nə repɔ̃   pɑ/
There's no answer.

Bien, veuillez annuler l'appel.
/bjɛ̃ vœje   anyle   l apɛl/
O.K., then cancel the call.

(or)

La ligne est occupée.
/la liɲ   ɛt‿ɔkype/
The line is busy.

Je retéléphonerai plus tard.
/ʒə rətelefɔnre   ply taːr/
I'll call back later.

REMARQUES

To send a telegram by phone, dial 14 (in Paris) and ask for
the operator; or you may send the telegram from the post office.

It is often difficult to get the number you are dialing, and Information and Assistance are usually busy. For Information in Paris, dial 12; for Assistance, dial 13.

There are several kinds of telephone books arranged by name, street, or profession.

You may make a direct call to the U.S. by dialing 19 – 1 – plus the area code and local number.

5
Divertissements et excursions

Entertainment and Excursions

Au café

At the Café

J'ai très soif, entrons dans ce café.
/ʒe trɛ swaf ɑ̃trɔ̃   dɑ̃   s(ə) kafe/
I'm very thirsty, let's go into this café.

Où préférez-vous vous asseoir, sur la terrasse ou à l'intérieur?
/u prefere vu   vuz‿aswaːr   syr la tɛras   u a lɛ̃terjœːr/
Where would you like to sit, on the terrace or inside?

Sur la terrasse. Nous pourrons regarder passer les gens.
/syr la tɛras   nu   purɔ̃   rəgarde pase   le ʒɑ̃/
On the terrace. We'll be able to watch people go by.

Garçon, s'il vous plaît!
/garsɔ̃   si(l) vu   plɛ/
Waiter, please!

Messieurs?
/mɛsjø/
    Yes?

Je voudrais un express/un petit crême/un grand crême/et un
/ʒə vudrɛ(z)   œ̃   ɛksprɛs œ̃ pti   krɛm œ̃ grɑ̃   krɛm e œ̃
croissant.
krwasɑ̃/
    *I'd like an expresso coffee/a small regular coffee/a large
    regular coffee/and a croissant.*

Moi, un demi et un sandwich au jambon.
/mwa œ̃ dmi e œ̃ sãdviʃ   o ʒãbɔ̃/
A draft beer and a ham sandwich for me.

Voilà, messieurs.
/vwala mɛsjø/
Here you are.

Garçon, l'addition s'il vous plaît.
/garsɔ̃   ladisjɔ̃   si(l) vu   plɛ/
Waiter, check please.

Le prix est indiqué sur le ticket.
/lə pri ɛt‿ẽdike   syr lə tikɛ/
The price is (indicated) on the tab.

Le service est ~~compris?~~ *inclus*
/lə sɛrvis   ɛ   kɔ̃pri/
Is the tip included?

Oui, monsieur.
/wi   məsjø/
Yes sir.

Merci.
/mɛrsi/
Thank you.

REMARQUES

The café in France is a national institution. Almost everywhere you will find cafés with outdoor terraces that are enclosed in winter (better known as sidewalk cafés).

Cafés are open generally from 7 to 2 A.M.; you may have breakfast, sandwiches, and often lunch. At any hour coffee, fruit juices, sodas, and alcoholic drinks are served. The café is a very important part of French life — a place to meet friends, to talk or rest, and to watch passers-by.

Au musée

At the Museum

REMARQUES

Museums are normally closed on Tuesdays and sometimes on Sunday mornings outside of Paris. They are open from 10 A.M. to 5 P.M.; in smaller cities they are closed from noon to 2 P.M. Big museums have guided tours in several languages or provide cassette recordings. In large cities, at the *Tourist Information Center* (**Syndicat d'initiative**), you will find publications advertising exhibits, special programs, etc.

■ **Quelques musées à Paris**   *Some museums in Paris*

Musée de l'Armée   Hôtel des Invalides, esplanade des Invalides (métro Latour-Mauborg, Varenne). 555.92.30.

Musée d'Art Moderne de la Ville de Paris   11, avenue du Président Wilson. 723.61.27. (métro Alma).

Musée des Arts Décoratifs   107-109, rue de Rivoli (métro Palais-Royal). 260.32.14.

Grand Palais (galeries nationales) avenue Winston-Churchill (métro Champs-Elysées-Clemenceau). 231.81.24.

Hôtel des Invalides   esplanade des Invalides. 555.92.30. (métro Latour-Maubourg, Varenne).

Musée de l'Homme   Palais de Chaillot (métro Trocadéro). 727.74.46.

Musée du Louvre (métro Palais-Royal et Louvre). 260.39.26 (buffet, salon de thé).

Musée de la Marine   Palais de Chaillot, pl. et métro Trocadéro. 727.96.51.

Orangerie des Tuileries jardins des Tuileries, côté Seine. 073.99.48.
(métro Concorde).
Palais de la Découverte avenue Franklin Roosevelt (métro
F.D.-Roosevelt). 359.16.65.
Musée Grévin 10, bld. Montmartre (métro Montmartre).
770.85.05.
Versailles Château et musée. 950.58.32. T.l.j. sf lundi de 10 h à
17 h.

Quelle est l'heure d'ouverture/de fermeture du musée?
/kɛl ɛ lœr duvɛrtyːr də fɛrmətyːr dy myze/
What time does the museum open/close?

Nous fermons à 17 h.
/nu fɛrmɔ̃ a disɛt‿œːr/
We close at 5 P.M.

Combien coûte l'entrée?
/kɔ̃bjɛ̃ kut lɑ̃tre/
What is the entrance fee?

Dix francs, monsieur.
/di frɑ̃ məsjø/
Ten francs sir.

Y a-t-il une réduction pour les enfants/les groupes?
/j a t il yn redyksjɔ̃ pur lez‿ɑ̃fɑ̃ le grup/
Is there a reduced rate for children/groups?

Les groupes de plus de dix personnes.
/le grup də ply də di pɛrsɔn/
For groups of more than ten.

Où peut-on acheter un catalogue en anglais?
/u pøt‿ɔ̃ aʃte œ̃ katalɔg ɑ̃‿ɑ̃glɛ/
Where can we find a catalogue in English?

Ici. En voici un.
/isi ɑ̃ vwasi œ̃/
Here's one.

Est-il permis de   prendre des photos?
/ɛtil pɛrmi d(ə) prɑ̃ːdr   de fɔto/
Are we allowed to take photographs?

Non, vous devez laisser votre appareil à l'entrée.
/nɔ̃ vu   dəve lɛse   vɔtr aparɛj   a lɑ̃tre/
No, you have to leave your camera at the entrance.

Où se trouve la galerie des Impressionistes?
/u sə truv   la galri   dez‿ɛ̃prɛsjɔnist/
Where's the gallery with the Impressionists?

Au rez-de-chaussée. Demandez au gardien.
/o re d ʃose   dəmɑ̃de   o gardjɛ̃/
On the ground floor. Ask the security guard.

Merci beaucoup, madame.
/mɛrsi boku   madam/
Thank you very much.

Le cinéma et le théâtre

Movies and Theater

■ **Cinéma**   *Movies*

Voulez-vous aller au cinéma ce soir?
/vule   vuz‿ale   o   sinema   sə   swaːr/
Do you want to go to the movies tonight?

Je veux bien. Quel film donne-t-on?
/ʒə vø   bjɛ̃   kɛl   film   dɔn   t ɔ̃/
Sure. What's on (lit. " what movie are they showing ")?

Un   film   policier/un   western/une   comédie   musicale/   une
/œ̃   film   pɔlisje   œ̃   wɛstɛrn   yn   kɔmedi   myzikal   yn
comédie/ un film dramatique.
kɔmedi   œ̃ film dramatik/
A crime drama/a Western/a musical/a comedy/a drama.

Qui est le réalisateur?
/ki   ɛ   lə realizatœːr/
Who's the director?

François Truffaut.
/frɑ̃swa   tryfo/

Quelles sont les vedettes qui y jouent?
/kɛl   sɔ̃   le vdɛt   ki   i   ʒu/
Who's in it (lit. " what stars act in it ")?

Jean-Paul Belmondo et Catherine Deneuve.
/ʒɑ̃   pol bɛlmɔ̃do   e katrin   dənœv/

A quelle heure est la séance?
/a kɛl   œr   ɛ la seɑ̃ːs/
What time is the showing?

Ce soir à 8 h et 10 h 30.
/sə swaːr a ɥit‿œːr e diz‿œr trɑ̃ːt/
Tonight at 8 and 10:30.

Trouverons-nous des billets?
/truvrɔ̃   nu de bijɛ/
Will we be able to get tickets?

Il faudra faire la queue.
/il fodra fɛr   la kø/
We'll have to stand in line.

J'aimerais mieux la séance de huit heures.
/ʒɛmrɛ   mjø   la seɑ̃ːs   də ɥit‿œːr/
I'd prefer the eight o'clock show.

Oui, cela finira vers 10 h   30   et nous irons souper.
/wi   sla finira vɛr diz‿œr trɑ̃ːt e nuz‿irɔ̃   supe/
*Yes, it'll end around 10:30, and then we can go and have
dinner.*

■ **Théâtre**   *Theater*

A quel théâtre joue-t-on la nouvelle pièce de Ionesco?
/a kɛl   teɑtr   ʒu t ɔ̃ la nuvɛl   pjɛs də iɔnɛsko/
Which theater is Ionesco's new play on at?

Au Théâtre de l'Odéon.
/o teɑtr   də lodeɔ̃/
The Théâtre de l'Odéon.

Allons réserver deux places.
/alɔ̃   rezɛrve dø   plas/
Let's go and reserve two seats.

■ **Au théâtre**   *At the theater*

Je désire réserver deux places pour la représentation de mardi
/ʒə dezir rezɛrve dø   plas   pur la rəprezãtasjɔ̃   də mardi

soir.
swaːr/

> *I want to reserve two seats for the Tuesday night perform-
> ance.*

Je regrette, c'est complet.
/ʒə r(ə)grɛt sɛ   kɔ̃plɛ/

> *I'm sorry, it's sold out.*

Et pour mercredi?
/e pur   mɛrkrədi/

> *What about Wednesday?*

Voulez-vous des places à l'orchestre ou au balcon?
/vule   vu   de plas   a lɔrkɛstr   u o balkɔ̃/

> *Would you like orchestra seats or balcony?*

Combien coûtent les places au balcon?
/kɔ̃bjɛ̃   kut   le plas   o balkɔ̃/

> *How much are the balcony seats?*

Trente francs.
/trãt   frã/

> *Thirty francs.*

Alors à l'orchestre, pas trop en arrière, quelque part au milieu.
/alɔːr a lɔrkɛstr   pɑ trop‿ã arjɛːr   kɛlkə   paːr o miljø/

> *Then orchestra seats, but not too far back, somewhere in the
> center.*

■ **Le soir de la pièce**   *The night of the play*

Où se trouve le vestiaire?
/u sə truv   lə vɛstjɛr/

> *Where is the cloakroom?*

Au fond du couloir à gauche.
/o fɔ̃   dy kulwaːr a goʃ/
At the end of the hallway on the left.

Puis-je avoir vos billets.
/pɥiʒ   avwaːr vo bijɛ/
May I have your tickets please.

Les voici.
/le vwasi/
Here they are.

Je voudrais un programme.
/ʒə vudrɛ(z) œ̃ prɔgram/
I'd like a program.

Bien monsieur, voici vos fauteuils.
/bjɛ̃ məsjø   vwasi vo fotœːj/
Sir, here are your seats.

Y a-t-il un entr'acte?
/j a t il œ̃n‿ɑ̃trakt/
Is there an intermission?

Oui monsieur dans une heure environ.
/wi məsjø dɑ̃z‿ yn‿ œːr ɑ̃virɔ̃/
Yes sir, in about an hour.

REMARQUES

1. At newsstands in cities you can buy a magazine with the times and prices of what's playing each week at the movies or the theater. In Paris it's called *Pariscope*. Reservations are recommended for plays. The afternoon performance is called **une matinée** /matiné/; the evening performance is called **une soirée** /sware/.

2. At the theater and the movies you will be shown to your seat by an usher (**une ouvreuse** /uvrœːz/) who will expect a tip: 1 franc at the movies, 3 to 5 at the theater.

Dans une boîte de nuit

Night clubs

REMARQUES

Discotheques have recorded music only, whereas certain night clubs and cabarets have live music and sometimes shows with dancers, comedians, magicians, etc.

In big night clubs you may have dinner with the show.

■ **Night clubs**   *Night clubs*

		Métro
Crazy horse	12 avenue Georges V	Etoile
Casino de Paris	16 avenue de Clichy	Trinité
Lido	78 Champs-Elysées	Georges V
Moulin-rouge	place Blanche	Blanche

■ **Clubs et discothèques**   *Clubs and discotheques*

Le Roméo (jazz)	4 rue de la Huchette	St. Michel
Riverside Club (young adults)	7 rue Grégoire de Tours	Odéon
Stéréo Club	6 rue Arsène Houssaye	Franklin-Roosevelt
Barbary Coast Saloon	11 rue Jules-Chaplain	Odéon

■ **Clubs privés à la mode**   *Fashionable private clubs*

Chez Régine
Au New Jimmy's
Chez Castel

Mademoiselle, pouvez-vous me recommander une boîte de
/madəmwazɛl   puve   vu   mə   r(ə)kɔmɑ̃de   yn   bwat   də

nuit?
nɥi/

> *Could you recommend a night club?*

Pour danser ou écouter de la musique?
/pur dɑ̃se   u   ekute   d   la   myzik/

> *To dance or to listen to music?*

J'aime mieux danser.
/ʒɛm   mjø   dɑ̃se/

> *I prefer to dance.*

Alors vous pouvez aller au Riverside Club.
/alɔːr vu   puvez‿ale   o/

> *Well, you can go to the Riverside Club.*

Combien cela coûte-t-il?
/kɔ̃bjɛ̃   sla   ku   t il/

> *How much does it cost?*

Trente francs, mais vous avez droit à une consommation.
/trɑ̃t   frɑ̃   mɛ   vuz‿ave   drwa a y yn   kɔ̃sɔmɑsjɔ̃/

> *Thirty francs, but that includes one drink.*

Quelle est l'ambiance?
/kɛl   ɛ   lɑ̃bjɑ̃ːs/

> *What kind of a place is it?*

C'est très agréable; vous serez assis à une petite table autour
/sɛ   trɛz‿agreabl   vu   srez‿asi   a yn   ptit   tabl   otur

de la piste de danse.
də la   pist   də   dɑ̃ːs/

> *It's really nice; you get to sit at a small table near the dance
> floor.*

Doit-on mettre une cravate pour y aller?
/dwat ɔ̃ mɛtr yn kravat pur i ale/
Do you have to wear a tie to get in?

Cela n'est pas obligatoire, mais beaucoup de gens en portent.
/sla nɛ paz‿ɔbligatwaːr mɛ boku d ʒɑ̃ ɑ̃ pɔrt/
You don't have to, but a lot of people do.

Et les femmes?
/e le fam/
What about the women?

Les femmes ne sont pas en robe longue, mais quand même
/le fam nə sɔ̃ paz‿ɑ̃ rɔb lɔ̃g mɛ kɑ̃ mɛm
assez élégantes.
asez‿elegɑ̃t/
Women aren't in long dresses, but still, they're quite elegant.

Et vous, aimez-vous danser?
/e vu ɛme vu dɑ̃se/
Do you like to dance?

Oui beaucoup.
/wi boku/
Yes very much.

Voulez-vous m'y accompagner?
/vule vu mi akɔ̃paɲe/
Would you like to come with me?

Avec plaisir; passez me chercher ce soir vers 21 h.
/avɛk plɛzir pase mə ʃɛrʃe sə swaːr vɛːr vɛ̃ te yn œːr/
Love to; pick me up tonight around nine.

■ **Fumer avec des amis**   *Smoking with friends*

Voulez-vous une cigarette?
/vule   vu   yn   sigarɛt/
Would you like a cigarette?

Avez-vous du feu s'il vous plaît?
/ave   vu   dy fø   si(l) vu   plɛ/
Do you have a light?

Est-ce que la fumée vous dérange?
/ɛ   s   kə   la fyme   vu   derɑ̃ːʒ/
Does the smoke bother you?

Puis-je avoir un cendrier?
/pɥi   ʒ   avwaːr   œ̃   sɑ̃drije/
May I have an ashtray?

Les cigarettes françaises sont trop fortes.
/le   sigarɛt   frɑ̃sɛz   sɔ̃   tro   fɔrt/
French cigarettes are too strong.

Non, merci je ne fume pas.
/nɔ̃   mɛrsi   ʒə n   fym   pɑ/
No thank you, I don't smoke.

Les jours fériés

Holidays

January 1   **Jour de l'An**   /ʒuːr də lɑ̃/   New Year's Day
April   **lundi de Pâques**   /lœ̃di d pɑk/   Easter Monday
May 1   **Fête du Travail**   /fɛt dy travaːj/   May Day
May 8   **Victoire 45**   /viktwaːr karɑ̃t sɛ̃ːk/   Victory in Europe
May 27   **Ascension**   /asɑ̃sjɔ̃/   Ascension
June 6   **Pentecôte**   /pɑ̃tkot/   Whit Monday
July 14   **Fête Nationale**   /fɛt nɑsjɔnal/   National Holiday
August 15   **Assomption**   /asɔ̃psjɔ̃/   Assumption
November 1   **Toussaint**   /tusɛ̃/   All Saints' Day
November 11   **Armistice 18**   /armistis diz‿ɥit/   Armistice, 1918
December 25   **Noël**   /nɔɛl/   Christmas

■ **Noël**   *Christmas*

Joyeux Noël!
/ʒwajø nɔɛl/
   Merry Christmas!

Que faites-vous pour le réveillon?
/k(ə) fɛt   vu   pur   lə revɛjɔ̃/
   What are you doing Christmas Eve?

Rien; ma famille ne vit pas en France.
/rjɛ̃   ma famiːj   nə vi   pɑ   ɑ̃   frɑ̃ːs/
   Nothing; my family doesn't live in France.

Voulez-vous le   passer avec nous?
/vule   vu   l(ə) pɑse   avɛk nu/
Would you like to spend it with us?

Avec plaisir.
/avɛk plɛzir/
I'd like that very much.

Je passe Noël avec des amis.
/ʒə pɑs   nɔɛl   avɛk dez‿ami/
I'm spending Christmas with friends.

Je réveillonne en famille.
/ʒə revɛjɔn   ã famiːj/
*I'm spending (lit. " celebrating ") Christmas Eve with my
family.*

REMARQUES

1.   School vacations in the summer: from the end of
June to around September 15.

2.   *Santa Claus* is **le père Noël, papa Noël** /lə pɛːr papa nɔɛl/.

3.   At *New Year's* (**le Nouvel An** /lə nuvɛl ã/) people wish
each other *Happy New Year* (**Bonne Année** /bɔn ane/).

Le Quatorze Juillet

July Fourteenth

Voulez-vous me dire quelque chose de la fête du quatorze
/vule   vu   m(ə) diːr kɛlkə   ʃoːz   də la fɛt dy katɔrz
juillet?
ʒɥijɛ/
> *Will you tell me something about the holiday on July
> fourteenth?*

Eh bien, c'est notre fête nationale, en commémoration de la
/e bjɛ̃   sɛ   nɔtr fɛt nɑsjɔnal ɑ̃ kɔmemɔrɑsjɔ̃   d la
prise de la Bastille.
priz də la bastiːj/
> *Well, it's our national holiday, in commemoration of the
> taking of the Bastille.*

Oui, je sais. Mais je voudrais savoir ce qu'on fait particu-
/wi ʒə sɛ   mɛ   ʒə vudrɛ   savwaːr s(ə) kɔ̃   fɛ partiky
lièrement ce jour-là.
ljɛrmɑ̃   sə ʒuːr la/
> *Yes, I know. But I'd like to know what people specially do
> on that day.*

D'abord, la veille du quatorze, on passe une grande partie de
/dabɔːr   la vɛj dy katɔrz   ɔ̃ pɑs   yn grɑ̃d   parti d
la nuit à danser.
la nɥi a dɑ̃se/
> *First of all, on the thirteenth (lit. " the eve of the fourteenth "),
> they spend a great part of the night dancing.*

On organise des bals chez des amis?
/ɔ̃ ɔrganiz de bal ʃe dez ami/
Are dances organized in friends' homes?

Oh, non! On danse en pleine rue, et tout le monde s'amuse
/o nɔ̃ ɔ̃ dɑ̃s ɑ̃ plɛn ry e tu l(ə) mɔ̃d samyz
follement.
fɔlmɑ̃/
*Oh, no! People dance right in the street, and everybody has
a terrific time.*

Comment peut-on danser en pleine rue? Ça doit gêner la
/kɔmɑ̃ pøt ɔ̃ dɑ̃se ɑ̃ plɛn ry sa dwa ʒɛne la
circulation?
sirkylɑsjɔ̃/
*How can they dance in the middle of the street? That must
interfere with traffic?*

Pas du tout. Certaines rues sont barrées et on y dresse une
/pɑ dy tu sɛrtɛn ry sɔ̃ bare e ɔ̃ i drɛs yn
estrade pour les musiciens.
ɛstrad pur le myzisjɛ̃/
*It really doesn't (lit. " not at all "). Certain streets are
closed and a platform is set up for the musicians.*

Et dans la journée du quatorze, qu'est-ce qui se passe
/e dɑ̃ la ʒurne dy katɔrz k ɛ s ki s pɑs
d'intéressant?
dɛ̃terɛsɑ̃/
*And does anything interesting happen on the day of the
fourteenth?*

Il y a une grande revue militaire.
/i(l) j a yn grɑ̃d rəvy militɛːr/
There is a big military review.

Chez nous, en Amérique, les enfants aiment lancer des pétards
/ʃe   nu   ãn‿amerik   lez‿ãfã   ɛm   lãse   de   petaːr

et faire beaucoup de   bruit le jour du quatre juillet.
e   fɛr   boku   d(ə) brɥi   lə   ʒuːr   dy   katr   ʒɥijɛ/
> *At home, in America, children like to set off firecrackers*
> *and make a lot of noise on the Fourth of July.*

En France, ce sont les discours politiques qui font le plus
/ã   frãːs   sə   sɔ̃   le   diskuːr   pɔlitik   ki   fɔ̃   lə   ply

grand bruit.
grã   brɥi/
> *In France, it's the political speeches that make the most*
> *noise.*

Il   n'y a pas de feu d'artifice?
/i(l) n j a pɑ   d   fø   dartifis/
> *There are no fireworks?*

Oh, si. La fête du quatorze juillet se termine par un grand feu
/o   si   la fɛt   dy katɔrz   ʒɥijɛ   s   tɛrmin   par œ̃   grã   fø

d'artifice.
dartifis/
> *Oh, yes. The fourteenth of July holiday ends with a big*
> *(display of) fireworks.*

J'aimerais bien être en France ce jour-là.
/ʒɛmrɛ   bjɛ̃‿ɛtr   ã   frãːs   sə   ʒuːr   la/
> *I'd like to be in France that day.*

Noël

Christmas

Est-ce qu'on célèbre Noël en France comme en Amérique?
/ɛ s k ɔ̃ selɛbr nɔɛl ɑ̃ frɑ̃ːs kɔm ɑ̃n̮amerik/
> *Do people celebrate Christmas in France the way they do in America?*

A ce qu'on m'a dit, nous ne fêtons pas Noël en France avec
/a skɔ̃ ma di nu n(ə) fɛtɔ̃ pɑ nɔɛl ɑ̃ frɑ̃ːs avɛk
autant d'éclat que chez vous.
otɑ̃ dekla k(ə) ʃe vu/
> *From what I've been told, we don't make as much of Christmas in France as you do in your country.*

Nous autres[1] Américains, nous considérons Noël comme la
/nuz̮oːtrəz̮amerikɛ̃ nu kɔ̃siderɔ̃ nɔɛl kɔm la
plus grande fête de l'année.
ply grɑ̃d fɛt də lane/
> *We Americans consider Christmas the most important holiday of the year.*

Chez nous Noël est avant tout une fête religieuse.
/ʃe nu nɔɛl ɛt̮ avɑ̃ tu yn fɛt rəliʒøz/
> *With us Christmas is mainly a religious celebration.*

En Amérique elle est devenue une institution commerciale de
/ɑ̃n̮amerik ɛl ɛ dəvny yn ɛ̃stitysjɔ̃ kɔmɛrsjal də

---

[1] **autres** is sometimes used with **nous** and **vous** for emphasis.

premier ordre.
prəmjɛr ɔrdr/
    In America it's become a first-class commercial institution.

Mais n'est-elle pas   aussi, comme en France, une occasion de
/mɛ nɛt‿ɛl pɑ(z) osi   kɔm ɑ̃ frɑ̃:s yn ɔkazjɔ̃ də
réjouissance pour les membres de la famille et pour leurs amis?
reʒwisɑ̃:s   pur le mɑ̃:br   də la fami:j e pur lœ:rz‿ami/
    But it's also an occasion for members of the family and their
    friends to get together, the same as in France, isn't it?

Oui, sans doute. Mais pendant tout le mois de décembre
/wi sɑ̃   dut   mɛ pɑ̃dɑ̃   tu   l(ə) mwɑ d desɑ̃:br
les magasins font des chiffres d'affaires énormes.
le magazɛ̃ fɔ̃ de ʃifr   dafɛrz‿enɔrm/
    Yes, definitely. But the stores do an enormous business the
    whole month of December.

Qu'est-ce qu'on vend spécialement à cette occasion?
/k e s kɔ̃ vɑ̃ spesjalmɑ̃ a sɛt ɔkazjɔ̃/
    What is sold especially at that time?

Toutes sortes de cadeaux et des quantités de cartes de Noël.
/tut   sɔrt də kado   e de kɑ̃tite   d kart də nɔɛl/
    All kinds of gifts and piles of Christmas cards.

En France aussi.
/ɑ̃ frɑ̃:s osi/
    In France it's the same.

Mais vous avez des arbres de Noël comme en Amérique?
/mɛ vuz‿ave dez‿arbr də nɔel kɔm   ɑ̃n amerik/
    But don't you have Christmas trees the way we have in
    America?

Dans certaines familles, oui. Mais cette coutume n'est pas
/dɑ̃ sɛrtɛn   fami:j wi mɛ   sɛt kutym nɛ pɑ

très répandue en France.
trɛ repɑ̃dy   ɑ̃ frɑ̃ːs/

> *In certain families, yes. But that custom isn't very wide-spread in France.*

Et les enfants, est-ce qu'ils ne reçoivent pas des cadeaux de
/e lez‿ɑ̃fɑ̃   e s kil   nə rəswav   pɑ de kado   d

Noël?
nɔɛl/

> *And don't the children get Christmas presents?*

Si; on leur offre quelques jouets, des poupées, des bonbons.
/si ɔ̃ lœːr ɔfr kɛlkə   ʒwɛ   de pupe   de bɔ̃bɔ̃/

> *Yes; they're given a few toys, some dolls, and candy.*

Mais, dites-moi donc, en France on ne fait rien de spécial
/mɛ   dit   mwa dɔ̃k   ɑ̃ frɑ̃ːs   ɔ̃ n fɛ   rjɛ̃   də spesjal

pour la fête de Noël?
pur   la fɛt   də nɔɛl/

> *But (tell me) don't they do anything special in France for Christmas?*

Ah, si. Nous avons le réveillon.
/ɑ   si   nuz‿avɔ̃   lə revɛjɔ̃/

> *Oh, yes. We have the* réveillon.

Qu'est-ce que c'est que le réveillon?
/k ɛ s kə se   k lə revɛjɔ̃/

> *What's the* réveillon?

Eh bien, c'est un souper qu'on sert dans la nuit de Noël.
/e bjɛ̃   sɛt‿œ̃ supe   kɔ̃   sɛr dɑ̃   la nɥi d nɔɛl/

> *Well, it's a supper that's served on Christmas Eve.*

Et en quoi consiste ce souper?
/e ¦ɑ̃ kwa kɔ̃sist sə supe/
And what do people have then (lit. " what does that supper consist of ")?

Des huitres sont de rigueur, puis de la dinde, une bûche de
/dez‿ɥitr sɔ̃ d(ə) rigœːr pɥi də la dɛ̃ːd yn byʃ də
Noël, et naturellement du champagne.
nɔɛl e natyrɛlmɑ̃ dy ʃɑ̃paɲ/
You can't do without oysters, then there's a roast turkey, then a special cake, and naturally champagne.

Mais est-ce qu'on ne se   souhaite pas un «*Merry Christmas*»?
/mɛ ɛ s kɔ̃ nə s(ə) swɛt paz‿œ̃/
But don't people wish one another a " Merry Christmas "?

Non. Cela n'est pas non plus une coutume française.
/nɔ̃ sla nɛ pɑ nɔ̃ ply yn kutym frɑ̃sɛːz/
Cependant, si on envoie une carte de Noël à quelqu'un, on y
səpɑ̃dɑ̃ si ɔ̃‿ɑ̃vwa yn kart də nɔɛl a kɛlkœ̃ ɔ̃‿i
met d'habitude: Joyeux Noël!
mɛ dabityd ʒwajø nɔɛl/
No. That's not a French custom either. But if you send a Christmas card to someone, you generally write: Joyeux Noël!

Je m'étonne qu'on ne se fasse pas des cadeaux comme chez
/ʒə metɔn kɔ̃ n sə fas pɑ de kado kɔm ʃe
nous.
nu/
I'm surprised that you don't exchange gifts the way we do.

Il n'y a pas de quoi s'étonner. D'après ce qu'on m'a
/i(l) n j a pɑ t kwa sətɔne daprɛ s kɔ̃ ma
dit, en Amérique les cadeaux de Noël sont une obligation
di ɑ̃‿amerik le kado d nɔɛl sɔ̃t‿yn ɔbligasjɔ̃

sociale plutôt qu'un plaisir.

sɔsjal   plyto kœ̃   plɛzir/

> *There's nothing to be surprised about. According to what I've been told, Christmas gifts in America are a social obligation rather than a pleasure.*

C'est vrai. Vous n'avez pas idée de la peine qu'on se

/sɛ   vrɛ   vu   nave   pɑ ide   d la pɛn   kɔ̃   s(ə)

donne pour se faire des douzaines de cadeaux.

dɔn   pur   sə fɛːr de duzɛn   də kado/

> *That's true. You have no idea what a pain it is to exchange dozens of gifts.*

Et à qui donc offre-t-on tout cela?

/e a ki dɔ̃k ɔfr   tɔ̃ tu   sla/

> *And who do people give presents (lit. " all that ") to?*

Aux parents, aux amis, aux patrons, aux employés, à toutes

/o   parɑ̃   oz‿ami o   patrɔ̃   oz‿ɑ̃plwaje   a tut

sortes de gens à tort et à travers.

sɔrt   də ʒɑ̃   a tɔr   e a travɛr/

> *Relatives, friends, employers, employees, all kinds of people without rhyme or reason.*

C'est un peu comme cela chez nous pour le Jour de l'An.

/sɛt‿œ̃ pø kɔm   sla ʃe   nu   pur lə ʒuːr də lɑ̃/

> *It's a bit like that with us on New Year's Day.*

Le Nouvel An

New Year's

Pour les Français la fête du Jour de l'An est plus importante
/pur le frãsε   la fεt dy ʒuːr də lã   ε   plyz ɛ̃pɔrtãt
que la Noël, n'est-ce pas?
kə la nɔεl nε s pɑ/
> *For the French, New Year's Day is more important than
> Christmas, isn't it?*

C'est que le Jour de l'An est une fête bien différente de celle
/sε   kə l(ə) zuːr də lã   εt yn fεt bjɛ̃ diferãt   də sεl
de Noël.
də nɔεl/
> *The fact is that New Year's Day is an absolutely different
> holiday from Christmas.*

En quoi donc ces deux fêtes diffèrent-elles principalement?
/ã kwa dɔ̃k se dø fεt difεr t εl   prɛ̃sipalmã/
> *How are the two holidays different, mainly?*

Eh bien, comme je vous le disais, la Noël est avant tout une
/e bjɛ̃ kɔm ʒə vu l dizε la nɔεl εt avã tu yn
fête religieuse. Mais le Jour de l'An est une fête sociale.
fεt rəliʒøz   mε l zuːr də lã   εt yn fεt sɔsjal/
> *Well, as I was telling you, Christmas is primarily a religious
> celebration. But New Year's is a social holiday.*

Que voulez-vous dire par une fête sociale?
/kə vulɛ vu diːr par yn fɛt sɔsjal/
What do you mean by a social holiday?

C'est qu'à cette occasion on observe certaines coutumes. Par
/sɛ k a sɛt ɔkazjɔ̃ ɔ̃n‿ɔbzɛrv sɛrtɛn kutym par
exemple, on fait de nombreuses visites.
ɛgzãpl ɔ̃ fɛ d nɔ̃brœz vizit/
*An occasion when certain social customs are observed. For
instance, people visit with each other a lot.*

Est-ce qu'on souhaite une bonne année comme chez nous en
/ɛ s kɔ̃ swɛt yn bɔn ane kɔm ʃe nu ãn‿
Amérique?
amerik/
*Do you wish one another a happy New Year the way we do
in America?*

Assurément. On dit: « Je vous souhaite une bonne année »,
/asyremã ɔ̃ di ʒə vu swɛt yn bɔn ane
ou simplement « Bonne Année! »
u sɛ̃pləmã bɔn ane/
*Oh yes. One says: " I wish you all the best " (lit. " a good
year "), or simply " Happy New Year! "*

Mais y a-t-il une façon spéciale de célébrer cette fête?
/mɛ j a t il yn fasɔ̃ spesjal də selebre sɛt fɛt/
But is there a special way to celebrate the holiday?

C'est surtout la veille du premier de l'An qui est une occasion
/sɛ syrtu la vɛːj dy prəmje d lã ki et‿yn ɔkazjɔ̃
de réjouissances.
d reʒwisãːs/
It's mainly New Year's Eve that's the time for parties.

Est-ce qu'à minuit on fait un grand vacarme comme chez nous
/ɛ s ka   minɥi ɔ̃ fɛt œ̃ grɑ̃ vakarm kɔm   ʃe   nu
en Amérique?
ɑ̃n‿amerik/
> *Do you make a lot of racket at midnight the way we do in*
> *America?*

Mais oui, et la veille du Nouvel An on va danser ou bien au
/mɛ wi e la vɛːj   dy nuvɛl   ɑ̃ ɔ̃ va dɑ̃se   u bjɛ̃ o
théâtre; puis vers minuit, comme à Noël, il y a un réveillon.
teɑtr   pɥi vɛr minɥi kɔm   a nɔɛl i(l) j a œ̃ revɛjɔ̃/
> *Oh yes, and on New Year's Eve we go to a dance or to the*
> *theater; then about midnight there's a* réveillon, *like*
> *Christmas.*

Vous me disiez qu'on faisait des cadeaux à l'occasion du
/vu   m(ə) dizje kɔ̃   fəzɛ   de kado   a lɔkazjɔ̃   dy
Premier de l'An.
prəmje d lɑ̃/
> *You told me that you gave presents on New Year's Day.*

En effet; entre parents et amis intimes on s'offre des étrennes.
/ɑ̃n‿efɛ ɑ̃tr   parɑ̃   e amiz‿ɛ̃tim   ɔ̃ sɔfr   dez‿etrɛn/
> *That's right; New Year's gifts are exchanged between*
> *relatives and close friends.*

Les jeux

Games

Voulez-vous jouer aux dames/aux échecs/aux cartes/au
/vule   vu   ʒwe   o   dam   oz‿eʃɛk   o   kart   o
jacquet?
ʒakɛ/
      Would you like to play checkers/chess/cards/backgammon?

Très volontiers, mais je ne me souviens plus des règles.
/trɛ vɔlɔ̃tje   mɛ ʒə n mə suvjɛ̃   ply de rɛgl/
      Sure, but I don't remember the rules.

Ce n'est pas grave, je vous apprendrai.
/s(ə) nɛ   pɑ grav ʒə vuz‿aprɑ̃dre/
      That's all right, I'll teach you.

■ **Echecs**　*Chess*

roi /rwa/ king
reine /rɛːn/ queen
tour /tuːr/ castle
fou /fu/ bishop
cheval /ʃval/ knight
pion /pjɔ̃/ pawn

■ **Cartes**　*Cards*

joker /ʒɔkɛr/ joker
as /ɑs/ ace

roi /rwa/ king
dame /dam/ queen
valet /valɛ/ jack
trèfle /trɛfl/ club
cœur /kœr/ heart
carreau /karo/ diamond
pique /pik/ spade

Une partie de cartes

A Game of Cards

Voulez-vous jouer au bridge avec Jeanne et moi?
/vule vu jwe o bridʒ avɛk ʒan   e mwa/
Would you like to play bridge with Jean and me?

Je veux bien, mais comment? Nous ne   sommes que trois.
/ʒə vø   bjɛ̃ mɛ kɔmɑ̃   nu n(ə) sɔm   kə trwɑ/
I'd be glad to, but how? There are only three of us.

Qu'est-ce que ça fait. On fera un mort.
/k es   kə sa fɛ   ɔ̃ fra œ̃ mɔːr/
What difference does that make? We'll have a dummy.

Alors, tirons au sort pour voir   qui donne.
/alɔːr tirɔ̃ o sɔːr pur vwaːr ki dɔn/
O.K., let's draw to see who deals.

A vous. C'est vous qui avez la carte la plus forte.
/a vu   sɛ   vu ki ave la kart la ply fɔrt/
You deal. You have the highest card.

Voilà. Les cartes sont battues. Voulez-vous couper?
/vwala le kart sɔ̃ baty   vule   vu kupe/
There. The cards are shuffled. Do you want to cut?

C'est fait. Allez-y.
/sɛ   fɛ   alez_i/
It's done. Go ahead.

Qui est-ce qui peut ouvrir?
/ki ɛ s ki pø uvriːr/
> *Who can open?*

Je passe.
/ʒə pɑs/
> *I pass.*

A vous de jouer.
/a vu də ʒwe/
> *It's your play.*

Pourquoi avez-vous joué atout avec votre roi de trèfle?
/purkwa ave vu zwe atu avɛk vɔtr rwa də trɛfl/
> *Why did you trump with your king of clubs?*

C'est bien simple. C'est parce que je ne pouvais pas jouer dans
/sɛ bjɛ̃ sɛ̃pl sɛ pars kə ʒə n puvɛ pɑ ʒwe dɑ̃
la couleur.
la kulœːr/
> *It's very simple. Because I couldn't follow suit.*

A vous. Ça va bien. Nous avons déjà gagné deux manches.
/a vu sa va bjɛ̃ nuz‿avɔ̃ deʒa gaɲe dø mɑ̃ʃ/
> *It's your play. We're doing fine. We've already won two
> hands.*

Combien de points avons-nous?
/kɔ̃bjɛ̃ d pwɛ̃ avɔ̃ nu/
> *What's the score (lit. " how many points do we have ")?*

Je ne sais pas. Mais nous avons tous les honneurs.
/ʒə n sɛ pɑ mɛ nuz‿avɔ̃ tu lez ɔnœːr/
> *I don't know. But we have all the honors.*

REMARQUES

1. For most of the games, the names are the same: **le bridge** /briʒ/; **la canasta** /kanasta/; **le gin rummy** /dʒin rɔmi/; **le whist** /wist/; **le poker** /pokɛːr/.

2. Additional vocabulary: **une levée** /ləve/, *trick*; **tricher** / triʃe/, *to cheat*; **un partenaire** /partənɛːr/, *partner*; **un adversaire** /advɛrsɛːr/ *opponent*; **c'est à refaire** /sɛt‿a r(ə)fɛːr/, *we must have another deal*; **quel est l'atout?** /kɛl ɛ latu/, *what are trumps?* **couper avec un atout** /kupe avɛk œ̃ atu/, *to trump* ; **une séquence** /sekɑ̃ːns/, *sequence*; **à qui de donner?** /a ki d(ə) dɔne/, *whose deal is it?* **à vous la donne!** /a vu la dɔn/, *your deal!* **une maldonne** /maldɔn/, *misdeal*.

Les sports

Sports

REMARQUES

Sports are almost as popular in France as in America. Important sports events are televised, and you can see games from all over Europe.

■ **Les sports les plus populaires**   *The most popular sports*

le football /lə futbɔl/ soccer
le rugby /lə rygbi/ rugby
le cyclisme /lə siklism/ bicycling
le ski /lə ski/ skiing
          aussi also
le basketball /lə baskɛtbɔl/ basketball

le handball /lə andbal/ handball
le tennis /lə tɛnis/ tennis
la natation /la natɑsjɔ̃/ swimming
atléthisme /atletism/ athletics
la boxe /la bɔks/ boxing

La bicyclette

The Bicycle

C'est à   vous cette bicyclette? Elle est toute neuve.
/sɛ   t‿a vu   sɛt bisiklɛt   ɛl   ɛ tut   nœːv/
Is that bicycle yours? It's really new.

Oui, je viens de l'acheter.   Comment la trouvez-vous?
/wi ʒə vjɛ̃ d laʃte   kɔmã   la truve   vu/
Yes, I've just bought it.   How do you like it?

Moi, vous savez, je ne m'y connais pas beaucoup.
/mwa vu   save   ʒə n mi kɔnɛ   pɑ bo‿ku/
Oh, I don't know much about bikes.

Je vous assure que c'est un bon vélo.   Essayez-le.
/ʒə vuz‿asyːr kə sɛt‿œ̃ bɔ̃ velo   ɛsɛje   lə/
I do (lit. " I can assure you "), and it's a good bike.   Try it.

La selle est trop haute.   Je peux à peine toucher les pédales.
/la sɛl ɛ   tro ot   ʒə pø   a pɛn tuʃe   le pedal/
The seat's too high.   I can hardly touch the pedals.

On peut la baisser.   On peut aussi baisser ou relever le guidon,
/ɔ̃ pø la bɛse   ɔ̃   pø(t) osi bɛse   u rəlve   l(ə) gidɔ̃
à volonté.
a vɔlɔ̃te/
      *It can be lowered.   You can also lower or raise the handle-
      bars to suit yourself (lit. " at will ").*

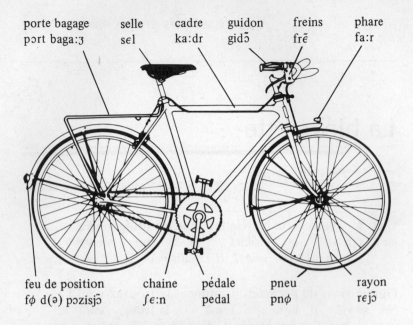

porte bagage   selle   cadre   guidon   freins   phare
pɔrt baga:ʒ   sɛl   ka:dr   gidɔ̃   frɛ̃   fa:r

feu de position   chaine   pédale   pneu   rayon
fø d(ə) pozisjɔ̃   ʃɛ:n   pedal   pnø   rɛjɔ̃

Vous savez, je n'ai plus l'habitude de monter à bicyclette.
/vu save ʒə ne ply labityd d mɔ̃te a bisiklɛt/
You know, I've forgotten how (lit. " I'm out of practice ")
to ride a bicycle.

Oh, ça ne s'oublie pas. Pourquoi n'en achèteriez-vous pas une,
/o sa n subli pɑ purkwa nɑ̃n aʃɛtərje vu pɑz‿yn
comme moi?
kɔm mwa/
Oh, you don't forget that kind of thing. Why don't you do
what I've done and buy one?

Ah, non. Mais je pourrais en louer une de temps en temps.
/ɑ nɔ̃ mɛ ʒə purɛ(z) ɑ̃ lwe yn də tɑ̃z‿ɑ̃ tɑ̃/
Oh, no. But I could rent one occasionally.

C'est parfait. On pourra ainsi faire de belles promenades à la
/sɛ parfɛ ɔ̃ pura ɛ̃si fɛːr də bɛl prɔmnad a la
campagne.
kɑ̃paɲ/
Fine. Then we can go on some nice trips in the country.

Le tennis

Tennis

Est-ce que vous aimez jouer au tennis?
/ɛ s kə vuz ɛme ʒwe o tɛnis/
Do you like to play tennis?

Oui, beaucoup; mais je joue très mal.
/wi boku   mɛ ʒə ʒu   trɛ mal/
Yes, very much; but I play very badly.

Voilà un court (de tɛnnis) qui me semble excellent.
/vwala ɑ̃ kuːr   də tɛnis   ki mə sɑ̃bl   ɛksɛlɑ̃/
That seems to be an excellent (tennis) court.

En effet. Le terrain semble en très bon état.
/ɑ̃n efɛ   lə tɛrɛ̃   sɑ̃bl   ɑ̃ trɛ bɔn eta/
It really is. The surface is in good condition.

Arrêtons-nous un instant pour regarder ces jeunes gens.
/arɛtɔ̃   nu   ɑ̃n ɛstɑ̃   pur rəgarde se ʒœn   ʒɑ̃/
Let's stop a minute to watch these (young) people.

Voyez comme cette jeune fille joue bien.
/vwaje kɔm   sɛt ʒœn fij ʒu bjɛ̃/
That girl really plays well.

Et elle sert avec beaucoup d'adresse.
/e ɛl   sɛr avɛk boku ·   dadrɛs/
And she has a really controlled serve.

La balle rase le filet.
/la bal   raz lə filɛ/
   The ball just grazes the net.

Mais le jeu de ce garçon n'est pas moins admirable.
/mɛ l(ə) ʒø d(ə) sə garsɔ̃ nɛ   pɑ mwɛ̃z admirabl/
   But that boy's game is terrific, too (lit. " is no less terrific ").

N'est-ce pas? Et son revers est formidable.
/nɛ   s pɑ   e sɔ̃ rəvɛr ɛ fɔrmidabl/
   Right. And his backhand is wonderful.

Voulez-vous faire une partie avec moi demain matin?
/vule   vu fɛr yn parti avɛk mwa dmɛ̃   matɛ̃/
   Will you play a game with me tomorrow morning?

Je veux bien. Mais je vous avertis que je suis un
/ʒə vø   bjɛ̃   mɛ   ʒ(ə) vuz‿avɛrti   kə ʒ sɥiz‿œ̃
joueur médiocre.
ʒwœːr medjɔkr/
   Glad to. But I warn you I'm only a fair player.

Vous êtes trop modeste. N'oubliez pas d'apporter la raquette
/vuz‿ɛt tro mɔdɛst   n ublije   pɑ dapɔrte   la rakɛt
et les balles.
e le bal/
   *You're just being modest. Don't forget to bring your racket
   and the balls.*

Je n'oublierai rien.
/ʒə n ublijere   rjɛ̃/
   I won't forget a thing.

REMARQUES

   1. **Servir** has the English meanings of *serve*, as in "They
were served coffee." and "a tennis serve." In particular, the verb

is used idiomatically in French: **à quoi sert cela?** /a kwa sɛr sla/, *what is that used for?* **de quoi vous servez-vous pour écrire?**/ də kwa vu sɛrve vu pur ekriːr/, *what do you use to write with?*

2. Additional sports vocabulary: **la barre fixe** /bar fiks/, *horizontal bar*; **la chasse** /ʃas/, *hunting*; **la course** /kurs/, *racing*; **l'escrime** /lɛskrim/ f., *fencing*; **en faveur de** /ɑ̃ favœːr də/, *in favor of*; **la glace** /glas/, *ice*; **le catch** /katʃ/, *wrestling*; **la marche** /marʃ/, *hiking*; **la natation** /natɑsjɔ̃/, *swimming*; **nager** /naʒe/, *to swim*; **le patin** /patɛ̃/, *skate*; **le patinage** /patinaʒ/, *skating*; **patiner** /patine/, *to skate*; **la piscine** /pisin/, *swimming pool*; **la piste** /pist/, *track*; **le terrain** /tɛrɛ̃/, *field*.

Le football

Soccer

Il   y a un match de football dimanche prochain au stade
/i(l) j a œ̃ matʃ   də futbɔl   dimɑ̃ʃ   prɔʃɛ̃   o stad
de   Colombes.
d(ə) kɔlɔ̃b/
> There's going to be a soccer game next Sunday at the
> Colombes Stadium.

Oui, je sais.   Je l'ai lu dans le journal.
/wi   ʒə sɛ   ʒə le ly dɑ̃ l ʒurnal/
> Yes, I know. I read it in the paper.

Si on y allait? Qu'est-ce que vous en dites?
/si ɔ̃n‿i alɛ   k ɛ s kə vuz‿ɑ̃ dit/
> How about going? What do you say?

Moi, j'irai volontiers. Qui est-ce qui joue?
/mwa ʒire vɔlɔ̃tje   ki ɛ s ki ʒu/
> Sure, I'll go. Who's playing?

C'est un match France–Angleterre.
/sɛt‿œ̃ matʃ frɑ̃ːs   ɑ̃glətɛːr/
> An English team against a French team.

Alors ça va être très disputé.
/alɔːr sa va ɛtr trɛ dispyte/
> Well, that'll be a very close game.

Sûrement. Je me demande quelle équipe va gagner.
/syrmã   ʒə m dəmãd   kɛl   ekip   va gaɲe/
It sure will. I wonder which team's going to win.

On dit que les Français sont très bien entraînés.
/ɔ̃ di k(ə) le frãsɛ   sɔ̃ trɛ bjɛ̃ nãtrɛne/
They say the French are in very good shape.

C'est possible. Mais les Anglais ont eu de belles victoires cette
/sɛ pɔsibl   mɛ lez‿ãglɛ   ɔ̃t‿ y d(ə)bɛl   viktwaːr sɛt
saison.
sɛzɔ̃/
*I guess so (lit. " that's possible "). But the English have
had some fine victories this season.*

N'oubliez pas que les Français les ont battus[1] il y a un an.
/n ublije pɑ k   le frãsɛ   lez‿ɔ̃ baty   i(l) j a œ̃n‿ã/
Don't forget that the French beat them a year ago.

Je sais. Mais depuis ils ont perdu leurs meilleurs joueurs.
/ʒə sɛ   mɛ dəpɥi ilz‿ɔ̃   pɛrdy lœr mɛjœr   ʒwœːr/
I know. But since then they've lost their best players.

Aucune importance; je suis sûr que les Français gagneront
/okyn   ɛ̃pɔrtãːs   ʒə sɥi syr kə le frãsɛ   gaɲərɔ̃
cette fois.
sɛt   fwa/
*That doesn't make any difference; I'm sure the French'll
win this time.*

Oui? Alors, combien voulez-vous parier?
/wi   alɔːr kɔ̃bjɛ̃   vule vu parje/
Yes? O.K., how much do you want to bet?

---

[1] from **battre**/batr/ § 38.

Cent francs. Mais vous avez perdu d'avance.
/sã   frã   mɛ   vuz‿ ave   pɛrdy d avãːs/
    A hundred francs. And you've lost already (lit. " you've lost
    in advance ").

REMARQUES

1. Note that **jouer** /ʒwɛ/, *to play*, is used with **à** when meaning "to play a game" and with **de** when meaning "to play an instrument": **jouez-vous du piano?** /ʒwɛ vu dy piano/, *do you play the piano?* **on joue au football** /ɔ̃ ʒu o futbɔl/, *we're playing soccer.*

2. Additional vocabulary for soccer: **un entraîneur** /ãtrɛnœːr/, *coach*; **le ballon** /balɔ̃/, *ball.*

La plage

The Beach

Où comptez-vous passer vos vacances?
/u kɔ̃te   vu   pɑse vo vakɑ̃ːs/
Where do you plan to spend your vacation?

J'irai probablement dans les Alpes. J'adore la montagne.
/ʒire prɔbabləmɑ̃   dɑ̃   lez‿alp   ʒ adɔːr la mɔ̃taɲ/
I'll probably go to the Alps. I love the mountains.

Moi, je préfère la plage. Je compte passer quelques
/mwa ʒ(ə) prefɛːr la plaʒ   ʒə kɔ̃t   pɑse   kɛlkə
semaines à Deauville.
smɛn   a dovil/
*I prefer the seashore. I expect to spend a few weeks at
Deauville.*

Je n'aime pas la mer. L'eau est trop froide. Et puis je ne
/ʒ(ə) nɛm   pɑ la mɛr lo   ɛ tro frwad e pɥi ʒə n
sais pas nager.
sɛ pɑ naʒe/
*I don't like the ocean. The water's too cold. And I don't
know how to swim, either.*

L'eau est un peu froide, c'est vrai. Mais on se réchauffe au
/lo   ɛt‿ œ̃ pø frwad sɛ   vrɛ   mɛ(z) ɔ̃ s reʃof   o
soleil.
sɔlɛːj/
*The water is a bit cold, you're right. But you warm up again
in the sun.*

Moi, j'attrape trop facilement des coups de soleil.
/mwa ʒatrap tro fasilmã de ku d sɔlɛːj/
I burn too easily.

C'est dommage. Moi, au contraire, j'aime être très bronzé.
/sɛ   dɔmaːʒ   mwa o kɔ̃trɛːr   ʒɛm   ɛtrə trɛ brɔ̃ze/
That's too bad. I (on the contrary) like to get a good tan.

Ce qui me convient le   mieux, c'est un petit coin tranquille à
/s ki mə kɔ̃vjɛ̃   l(ə) mjø   sɛ   t‿œ̃ pti kwɛ̃ trãkil   a

la campagne.
la kãpaɲ/
What suits me best is a nice quiet nook in the country.

Deauville est très vivant. On s'y amuse beaucoup. Moi,
/dovil   ɛ trɛ vivã   ɔ̃ si amyz boku   mwa

j'aime cette vie-là.
ʒɛm   sɛt vi la/
Deauville is very lively. You can have a lot of fun there.
I like that kind of life.

On y va moins pour prendre des bains de mer que pour jouer
/ɔ̃n‿i va mwɛ̃ pur prã:dr de bɛ̃ d mɛr kə pur jwe

au casino.
o kasino/
People go there not so much for the swimming as for the
gambling at the Casino.

Il est certain que le casino offre beaucoup d'amusements:
/il ɛ sɛrtɛ̃   k lə kasino ɔfr boku   damyzmã

danse, musique, jeu.
dã:s   myzik ʒø/
The Casino certainly offers several kinds of entertainment:
dancing, music, gambling.

Vous allez sans doute vous installer à l'hôtel?
/vuz‿ale   sã   dut   vuz‿ε̃stale   a l otεl/
You're going to stay at the hotel aren't you?

Non, j'ai loué une petite villa au bord de la mer.
/nɔ̃   ʒe lwe yn ptit   vila o bɔːr də la mεːr/
No, I've rented a cottage right on the shore.

Eh bien, je vous souhaite de bonnes vacances.
/e bjε̃   ʒ(ə) vu   swεt   də bɔn   vakɑ̃ːs/
Well, I hope you have a pleasant vacation.

REMARQUES

1.   You will find many beaches in France on the Mediterranean and Atlantic and on the English Channel. The water is warmer along the Mediterranean so that many more people are attracted to the Riveria than to the more northern beaches.

Well known for their beaches are: Nice, Cannes, Juan les Pins, and St. Tropez—all on the *Riviera* (**Côte d'Azur** /kot dazyr/); Biarritz and the Landes on the *Atlantic* (**Atlantique** /atlɑ̃tik/); and Brittany, which has beaches on the Atlantic and on the *English Channel* (**la Manche** /mɑ̃ʃ/).

Beaches are less crowded in June, at the end of August, and in early September.

2.   Some signs: **Plage Privée** /plaʒ prive/, *Private Beach*; **Baignade Interdite** /bεɲad ε̃tεrdit/, *No Swimming*; **Interdit aux Nudistes** /ε̃tεrdi o nydist/, *No Nude Bathing*.

3.   Some additional vocabulary: **le nageur** /naʒœːr/, *swimmer*; **patauger** /patoʒe/, *to splash about*; **plonger** /plɔ̃ʒe/, *to dive*; **le plongeon** /plɔ̃ʒɔ̃/, *dive*; **le maillot de bain** /majo d bε̃/, *bathing suit*; **la brassée** /brase/, *swimming stroke*; **la douche** /duʃ/, *shower*; **la serviette de bain** /sεrvjεt də bε̃/, *bath towel*.

Pour louer une villa

Renting a Villa

Je voudrais louer une villa pour la saison d'été.
/ʒə vudrɛ   lwe   yn vila pur la sɛzɔ̃ dete/
   I'd like to rent a villa for the summer season.

En montagne ou au bord de la mer?
/ɑ̃ mɔ̃taɲ   u o bɔːr də la mɛːr/
   In the mountains or at the seashore?

J'aimerais une plage tranquille, vous savez, un bon petit coin
/ʒɛmrɛ   yn plaʒ trɑ̃kil   vu   save   œ̃ bɔ̃ pti   kwɛ̃
pour familles.
pur fami:j/
   *I'd like a very quiet beach — you know, a nice little family
   spot.*

Combien de pièces vous faudrait-il?
/kɔ̃bjɛ̃   d pjɛs   vu   fodrɛt‿il/
   How many rooms would you need?

Il   nous faudrait au moins six pièces: deux chambres à cou-
/i(l) nu   fodrɛ   o mwɛ̃ si pjɛs   dø ʃɑ̃br   a ku-
cher une salle à manger, un salon, une cuisine et une petite
ʃe   yn sal a mɑ̃ʒe   œ̃ salɔ̃   yn kɥizin e yn ptit
chambre pour notre jeune fille au pair.
ʃɑ̃ːbr   pur nɔtr ʒœn fij o pɛːr/
   *We'd need at least six rooms: two bedrooms, a dining room,
   a living room, a kitchen, and a small room for our au pair.*

Nous avons une jolie villa à Etretat qui fera justement votre
/nuz‿avɔ̃   yn ʒɔli vila a etrəta ki fra ʒystəmã vɔtr
affaire.
afɛːr/
> *We have a nice villa at Etretat which will just suit you.*

A quelle distance se trouve-t-elle de la plage?
/a kɛl   distãːs sə truv t ɛl də la plaːʒ/
> *How far is it from the beach?*

C'est tout près, avec une vue splendide sur la Manche.
/sɛ tu prɛ avɛk yn vy splũdid   syr la mãʃ/
> *It's very close, with a very fine view of the Channel.*

La villa est complètement meublée, bien entendu?
/ la vila ɛ kɔ̃plɛtmã   mœble   bjɛ̃ n ãtãdy/
> *The villa is completely furnished, of course?*

Complètement, sauf le linge, que vous aurez vous-même à
/lɔ̃plɛtmã   sof lə lɛ̃ʒ   kə   vuz‿ɔre   vu   mɛm a
fournir.
furniːr/
> *Everything except linen, which you'll have to supply yourself.*

Comment la cuisine est-elle équipée?
/kɔmã   la kɥizin ɛt‿ ɛl   ekipe/
> *What are the kitchen appliances?*

Réfrigérateur, machine à laver la vaisselle, cuisinière électrique.
/refriʒeratœːr maʃin   a lave la vɛsɛl   kɥizinjɛːr elɛktrik/
> *Refrigerator, dishwasher, and electric range.*

C'est parfait. Et la salle de bain?
/sɛ parfɛ   e la sal də bɛ̃/
> *That's perfect. And what about the bathroom?*

Baignoire avec eau chaude courante.
/beɲwaːr avɛk o ʃod kurɑ̃t/
Bath with running hot water.

Quel est le prix du loyer pour la saison?
/kɛl ɛ lə pri dy lwaje pur la sɛzɔ̃/
What is the rent for the season?

Pour deux mois, c'est-à-dire du 15 juillet au 15 septembre,
/pur dø mwɑ sɛ t a diːr dy kɛ̃ːz ʒɥijɛ o kɛ̃ːz sɛptɑ̃br
c'est dix mille francs.
sɛ di mil frɑ̃/
*For two months — that is, from July 15 to September 15 —
it's ten thousand francs.*

Alors je préfère rester chez moi.
/alɔr ʒ(ə) prefɛːr rɛste ʃe mwa/
In that case I prefer to stay home.

Excursions

Excursions

Je voudrais aller en excursion à Chartres/en Bretagne.
/ʒə vudrɛ(z) ale ɑ̃n‿ɛkskyrzjɔ̃ a ʃartr ɑ̃ brətaɲ/
I would like to go on an excursion to Chartres/Brittany.

Adressez-vous à une agence de voyages.
/adrɛse vu a yn aʒɑ̃s də vwajaːʒ/
Go to a travel agency.

Y a-t-il un office de tourisme?
/j a t il œ̃n‿ɔfis də turism/
Is there a tourist center?

Certainement, ils vous conseilleront un tour guidé de la ville.
/sɛrtɛnmɑ̃ il vu kɔ̃sɛjərɔ̃ œ̃ tuːr gide d la vil/
Certainly, they will recommend a guided sightseeing tour of the city.

Où puis-je acheter un bon guide?
/u pɥi ʒ aʃete œ̃ bɔ̃ gid/
Where can I get a good guide?

Au bureau de renseignements.
/o byro d rɑ̃sɛɲmɑ̃/
At the information counter.

Le guide parle-t-il anglais?
/lə gid parl t il ɑ̃glɛ/
Does the guide speak English?

Vous pouvez en demander un si vous voulez.
/vu   puve(z) ɑ̃ dmɑ̃de   œ si vu   vule/
You may ask for one if you wish.

■ **Endroits à voir**   *Places to see*

aquarium /akwarjɔm/ aquarium
château /ʃɑto/ castle
cathédrale /katedral/ cathedral
mairie /meri/ city or town hall
église /egliːz/ church
jardins /ʒardɛ̃/ gardens
port /pɔːr/ harbor
monument /mɔnymɑ̃/ monument
musée /myze/ museum
parc /park/ park
centre commercial /sɑ̃tr(ə) kɔmɛrsjal/ shopping center
tour /tuːr/ tower
zoo /zoo/ zoo

A travers la France

Through France

Quelles sont les autres régions de France que je devrais visiter?
/kɛl   sɔ̃ lez‿otr   reʒjɔ̃   də frɑ̃ːs kə ʒ dəvrɛ   vizite/
What other regions of France should I visit?

Ecoutez: puisque vous comptez aller en Bretagne, passez donc
/ekute   pɥisk   vu   kɔ̃te   ale   ɑ̃ brətaɲ   pɑse   dɔ̃
par la Touraine.
par la turɛːn/
> *Hey, since you plan to go to Brittany, then go through*
> *Touraine.*

C'est là que se trouvent ces beaux châteaux, n'est-ce pas?
/sɛ   la k sə truv   se bo   ʃato   nɛ s   pɑ/
> *That's where all those beautiful châteaux are, isn't it?*

Mais oui, les châteaux de la Loire. Et puis, après avoir visité
/mɛ wi   le ʃato   d la lwaːr e pɥi aprɛz‿avwaːr vizite
la Bretagne, vous pourriez revenir par la Normandie.
la brətaɲ   vu   purje   rəvnir par la nɔrmɑ̃di/
> *Yes, the châteaux of the Loire. And then, after visiting*
> *Brittany, you could come back through Normandy.*

Ça, c'est une bonne idée. Oui, il faut absolument que je
/sa sɛt‿yn   bɔn   ide   wi   i(l) fo(t) absɔlymɑ̃   kə ʒ
fasse un tour en Normandie.
fas œ̃ tuːr ɑ̃ nɔrmɑ̃di/
> *That's a good idea. Yes, I really have to take a trip to*
> *Normandy.*

Vous avez raison. Vous aimerez les belles plages de la côte
/vuz‿ave rɛzɔ̃   vuz‿ɛmre   le bɛl   plaʒ də la kot

normande, Trouville, par exemple.
nɔrmɑ̃ːd   truvil   par ɛgzɑ̃ːpl/

> *You're right. You'll like the lovely beaches along the*
> *Normandy coast — Trouville for instance.*

Oui, il y a beaucoup à voir en France en été. Mais en
/wi i(l) j a bokup   a vwaːr ɑ̃ frɑ̃ːs   ɑ̃n‿ete mɛ(z) ɑ̃n

hiver, où pourrait-on aller?
‿iveːr u purɛt   ɔ̃ ale/

> *Yes, there's a great deal to see in France in the summer.*
> *But where could I go in winter?*

Aimez-vous les sports d'hiver?
/ɛme   vu   le spɔr d iveːr/

> *Do you like winter sports?*

Je n'en raffole pas. Cependant j'aime assez le ski.
/ʒə nɑ̃ rafɔl   pɑ səpɑ̃dɑ̃   ʒɛm ase l ski/

> *I'm not crazy about them. I suppose I like skiing (lit.*
> *" however, I like skiing well enough ").*

Dans ce cas, vous devriez passer quelques semaines à
/dɑ̃ s(ə) kɑ vu   dəvrije pɑse kɛlkə   smɛn   a

Chamonix.
ʃamɔni/

> *In that case, you ought to spend a few weeks at Chamonix.*

Chamonix? C'est dans les Alpes, ça, n'est-ce pas?
/ʃamɔni   sɛ   dɑ̃ lez‿alp   sa nɛs   pɑ/

> *Chamonix? That's in the Alps, isn't it?*

Oui, c'est une station d'hiver très fréquentée. Mais natu-
/wi sɛ t‿yn stasjɔ̃ d iveːr trɛ frekɑ̃te   mɛ naty-

rellement il faudra que vous alliez aussi sur la Côte d'Azur.

rɛlmã il fodra k vuz‿alje osi syr la kot d azyr/

Yes, it's a great winter resort. But naturally you'll also
have to go to the Riviera (or the Côte d'Azur).

J'espère que oui. Le climat du midi doit être bien agréable.

/ʒ ɛspɛːr kə wi lə klima dy midi dwat ɛtr bjẽn agreabl/

I hope so. The southern climate must be very pleasant.

Très agréable. Que ce soit à Cannes, à Nice ou à Menton,

/trɛ z‿agreabl kə s(ə) swa(t) a kan a nis u a mãtɔ̃

il fait un temps très doux, et le paysage est de toute beauté.

il fɛt‿ œ̃ tã trɛ du e l pɛizaʒ ɛ də tut bote/

Very pleasant. Cannes, Nice, Menton — wherever you go —
the climate is very mild, and the scenery is really beautiful.

La Bretagne

Brittany

On m'a conseillé de faire un tour en Bretagne cet été. Con-
/ɔ̃ ma kɔ̃sɛje d fɛr œ̃ tur ɑ̃ brətaɲ sɛt ete kɔn-
naissez-vous cette région?
ɛse   vu sɛt reʒjɔ̃/
> *I was advised to take a trip to Brittany this summer. Do you
> know that region?*

Mais oui, très bien. J'y ai passé plusieurs étés bien agréables.
/mɛ wi trɛ bjɛ̃   ʒ i e pɑse plyzjœrz ete bjɛ̃ agreabl/
> *Oh yes, very well. I've spent several very pleasant summers
> there.*

Qu'est-ce qu'il y a de particulièrement intéressant en cette
/k ɛ s ki(l) j a d partikyljɛrmɑ̃   ɛ̃terɛsɑ̃   ɑ̃ sɛt
région?
reʒjɔ̃/
> *What's specially interesting in the area?*

Le paysage, les gens, les coutumes, tout y est différent du reste
/lə pɛizaʒ le ʒɑ̃ le kutym   tut i ɛ diferɑ̃   dy rɛst
de la France.
də la frɑ̃ːs/
> *The scenery, the people, the customs — everything's
> different from the rest of France.*

Je n'ai jamais compris pourquoi ce pays s'appelle la Bretagne.
/ʒə ne ʒamɛ kɔ̃pri purkwa s pɛi s apɛl   la brətaɲ

Est-ce que vous le savez?
ɛ s   kə vu   lə save/
> I've never understood why Brittany is called that. Do you
> know?

C'est parce que les Bretons sont originaires de la Grande
/sɛ   pars kə   le brətɔ̃   sɔ̃   t‿ɔriʒinɛːr də la grɑ̃d
Bretagne.
brətaɲ/
> Because the Bretons originally came from Great Britain.

Vraiment? Je ne savais pas ça. Quand donc ont-ils quitté leur
/vrɛmɑ̃   ʒə n save   pɑ sa kɑ̃   dɔ̃ːk ɔ̃ t‿il kite lœːr
pays d'origine?
pɛi d ɔriʒin/
> Really? I didn't know that. So when did they leave their
> original country?

A l'époque des invasions anglo-saxonnes, c'est-à-dire vers le
/a l epɔk   dez‿ɛ̃vazjɔ̃   z‿ɑ̃glosaksɔn   sɛt a diːr vɛr lə
cinquième siècle.
sɛ̃kjɛm   sjɛkl/
> At the time of the Anglo-Saxon invasions — about the fifth
> century.

Mais alors, les Bretons sont de race celtique?
/mɛ(z) alɔːr le brətɔ̃   sɔ̃   d ras sɛltik/
> Then the Bretons are Celtic (lit. " of Celtic race ")?

Oui, comme les Irlandais ou les Gallois.
/wi kɔm   lez‿irlɑ̃dɛ   u le galwa/
> Yes, like the Irish or the Welsh.

Quelle langue parlent-ils?
/kɛl   lɑ̃ːg   parl t il/
> What language do they speak?

Une langue spéciale qu'on appelle le   breton.
/yn   lã:g   spesjal   kɔ̃n‿apɛl   l(ə) brətɔ̃/
A special language called Breton.

A quoi ressemble cette langue?
/a kwa rəsãbl   sɛt lã:g/
What other language is it like?

Elle ressemble beaucoup au gallois.
/ɛl   rəsãbl   boku   o   galwa/
It's very like Welsh.

Alors, les Bretons ne   parlent pas français?
/alɔ:r   le brətɔ̃   n(ə) parl   pɑ frãsɛ/
So the Bretons don't speak French?

Mais si, ils parlent les deux langues.
/mɛ   si il parl   le dø   lã:g/
Oh yes, they speak both languages.

On m'a parlé aussi des pardons de Bretagne, mais je ne sais
/ɔ̃   ma parle osi   de pardɔ̃   də brətaɲ   mɛ   ʒə n sɛ
pas exactement ce que c'est.
pɑ z‿egzaktəmã   s kə sɛ/
I was also told about the pardons (*pilgrimages*) *in Brittany,*
but I don't exactly know what they are.

Un pardon est une sorte de pèlerinage à la chapelle d'un saint
/œ̃   pardɔ̃   ɛt‿yn sɔrt də pɛlrinaʒ   a la ʃapɛl   d œ̃ sɛ̃
local, et c'est aussi l'occasion de réjouissances populaires.
lɔkal e sɛt‿osi   l ɔkazjɔ̃   d reʒwisã:s   pɔpylɛ:r/
A pardon *is a sort of pilgrimage to the chapel of some local*
saint, and it's also an occasion for general celebration.

Est-ce que les Bretons portent encore leurs costumes pitto-
/ɛ s   kə le brətɔ̃   pɔrt   ɑ̃kɔːr lœːr kɔ̃stym   pitɔ

resques?
rɛsk/

Do the Bretons still wear their picturesque costumes?

Surtout les gens de la campagne. Les femmes, en particulier,
/syrtu   le ʒɑ̃   d la kɑ̃paɲ   le fam   ɑ̃ partikylje

portent leurs jolies coiffes et leurs tabliers brodés.
pɔrt   lœːr ʒɔli   kwaf e lœːr tablije brɔde/

Specially the country people. The women, in particular,
wear their pretty headdresses and their embroidered aprons.

Ça doit être un pays bien intéressant. Il faut que j'aille y faire
/sa dwat ɛtr œ̃ pɛi bjɛ̃ n̰ɛterɛsɑ̃   i(l) fo k ʒaj   i fɛr

un tour cet été.
œ̃ tuːr sɛt ete/

It must be a very interesting part of the country. I'll have
to take a trip there this summer.

En automobile

Driving

Zut! nous serons bientôt en panne d'essence!
/zyt nu   srɔ̃   bjɛ̃to   ɑ̃ pan   d ɛsɑ̃ːs/
Drat! we'll soon be out of gas!

Eh bien, ce ne sera pas drôle d'avoir une panne ici.
/e bjɛ̃   sə n s(ə)ra pɑ drol d avwaːr yn   pan   isi/
Well, it won't be funny to get stuck here.

Il   nous reste à peine un litre.
/i(l) nu   rɛst a pɛn   œ̃ litr/
We have just about (lit. " barely ") a liter left.

Ralentissez. Il y a un poste d'essence devant nous.
/ralɑ̃tise   i(l) j a œ̃ pɔst d ɛsɑ̃ːs   dəvɑ̃ nu/
Slow down. There's a gas station ahead of us.

Quelle chance! Juste à temps. (L'auto s'arrête)
/kɛl   ʃɑ̃ːs   ʒyst a tɑ̃   lɔto   sarɛːt/
That's real luck! Just in time. (The car stops)

(A l'employé) Faites le plein, s'il vous plaît. Et vérifiez le
/a lɑ̃plwaje   fɛt   lə plɛ̃ si(l) vu   plɛ   e verifje l
niveau d'huile.
nivo   d ɥil/
(To the attendant) Fill it up, please. And check the oil.

(L'employé) Oui, monsieur. Et votre radiateur, faut-il y
/ lăplwaje wi məsjø e vɔtr radjatœːr fot͜ il i
mettre de l'eau?
mɛtr də lo/

> (*Attendant*) *Yes, sir. What about the radiator; does it need water?*

Merci. Je l'ai fait remplir avant de quitter Paris.
/mɛrsi ʒə le fɛ rãplir avã d kite pari/

> *No, thank you. I had it filled before I left Paris.*

Nos pneus sont en bon état, n'est-ce pas?
/no pnø sɔ̃ t͜ ã bɔn eta n ɛs pɑ/

> *Our tires are in good condition, right?*

Je crois que oui. Mais je ferai vérifier la pression d'air.
/ʒə krwa k(ə) wi mɛ ʒə fre verifje la prɛsjɔ̃ d ɛːr/

> *I think so. But I'll have the air pressure checked.*

Ce ne serait pas amusant d'avoir une crevaison en route.
/sə n srɛ pɑz͜ amyzã d avwaːr yn krəvɛzɔ̃ ã rut/

> *It wouldn't be much fun to get a flat tire on the way.*

Soyez tranquille. Nous avons un bon pneu de secours.
/swaje trãkil nuz͜ avɔ̃ œ̃ bɔ̃ pnø d səkur/

> *Don't worry. We have a good spare (tire).*

Et puis, ne conduisez pas si vite. La route est humide et on
/e pɥi nə kɔ̃dɥize pɑ si vit la rut ɛ t͜ ymid e ɔ̃
peut déraper.
pø derape/

> *And by the way, don't drive so fast. The road's wet and we might skid.*

N'ayez pas peur. Quand je suis au volant, il n'y a pas
/nɛje pɑ pœːr kã ʒ sɥiz͜ o vɔlã i(l) n j a pɑ
de danger.
d dãʒe/

> *Don't be afraid. When I'm at the wheel, there's no danger.*

Ça y est. Tout est prêt. On peut repartir.
/sa i ɛ   tut   ɛ prɛ   ɔ̃   pø   r(ə)partir/
All right. Everything's ready. We can start off.

Combien de kilomètres nous reste-t-il à faire?
/kɔ̃bjɛ̃   d kilomɛtr   nu   rɛst   il a fɛːr/
How many kilometers do we still have to go?

Une centaine. On arrivera à temps pour dîner.
/yn sɑ̃tɛn   ɔ̃n‿arivra   a tɑ̃   pur dine/
About a hundred. We'll get there in time for dinner.

Il commence à faire nuit. Il faudrait allumer les phares
/il kɔmɑ̃s   a fɛːr nɥi   i(l) fodrɛ(t) alyme   le far
(mettre les lumières).
 mɛtr   le lymjɛr/
It's beginning to get dark. We ought to put on our lights.

En effet; je ne voudrais pas écraser une vache.
/ɑ̃n‿efɛ   ʒə n vudrɛ   pɑ(z) ekraze yn vaʃ/
Right; I wouldn't want to hit a cow.

Et ces paysans conduisent toujours du mauvais côté.
/e se pɛizɑ̃   kɔ̃dɥiz   tuʒuːr   du mɔvɛ   kote/
And these peasants always drive on the wrong side.

Mais la route est bonne. On peut foncer.
/mɛ   la rut   ɛ bɔn   ɔ̃   pø   fɔ̃se/
But the road's good. We can speed up.

La côte est raide. Vous ne pourrez jamais la monter en
/la kot ɛ   rɛd   vu n pure   ʒamɛ   la mɔ̃te   ɑ̃
deuxième.
døzjɛm/
*The hill's steep. You'll never be able to make it in second
(gear).*

Si, mais je passerai en première pour ne pas fatiguer le
/si mɛ   ʒ(ə) pɑsre   ɑ̃ prəmjɛːr   pur   nə pɑ fatige   l
moteur.
mɔtœːr/
> *Yes, I could, but I'll shift into first so as not to strain the engine.*

Regardez donc ce poteau indicateur: Virage dangereux.
/rəgarde   dɔ̃k   sə poto   ɛ̃dikatœːr   viraːʒ   dɑ̃ʒrø/
> *Just look at that signpost: Dangerous Turn.*

Oui, oui, je vois. Je ferai bien attention.
/wi   wi   ʒə vwa   ʒə fre   bjɛ̃   n‿atɑ̃sjɔ̃/
> *Hey, yes, I see. I'll be really careful.*

Voilà une voiture qui vient. Klaxonnez!
/vwala yn vwatyːr ki vjɛ̃   klaksone/
> *Here comes a car. Blow your horn!*

Ces phares sont aveuglants. Et cet idiot-là fait du cent trente
/se faːr   sɔ̃   t‿avœglɑ̃   e sɛt‿idjo la fɛ   dy sɑ̃   trɑ̃ːt
à l'heure!
a lœːr/
> *The headlights are blinding. And that idiot is doing one hundred thirty (kilometers) an hour.*

On devrait bien lui retirer son permis de conduire.
/ɔ̃   dəvrɛ   bjɛ̃   lɥi r(ə)tire sɔ̃   pɛrmi d kɔ̃dɥiːr/
> *They ought to take his driver's license away from him.*

Ralentissez! nous entrons dans un village.
/ralɑ̃tise   nuz‿ɑ̃trɔ̃   dɑ̃z‿ œ̃ vilaʒ/
> *Slow down! We're coming into a village.*

Tiens! pourquoi tout ce monde au bord de la route?
/tjɛ̃   purkwa   tu   s mɔ̃d   o bɔːr də la rut/
> *Hey! Why are all those people at the side of the road?*

Je parie que c'est un accident.
/ʒə pari   k   sɛ   t‿œ̃ n‿aksidɑ̃/
I bet it's an accident.

Si on s'arrêtait?[1] On pourra peut-être rendre service.
/si ɔ̃ sarɛtɛ   ɔ̃ pura   pøt‿ɛtr(ə) rɑ̃ːdr sɛrvis/
Should we stop? Perhaps we could help in some way.

(A un spectateur) Qu'est-ce qui est arrivé?
/ a œ̃ spɛktatœːr k e s ki ɛ t‿arive/
(To an onlooker) What happened?

(Le premier spectateur) Il paraît qu'ils ont été tamponnés par
/ lə prəmje spɛktatœːr i(l) parɛ ki(l)z‿ɔ̃ t ete tɑ̃pɔne   par
un camion.
œ̃ kamjɔ̃/
(The first bystander) They seem to have been rammed by a truck.

Il y a eu des victimes?
/i(l) j a y de viktim/
Was anyone hurt (lit. " were there any victims ")?

(Le premier spectateur) Les deux passagers, un monsieur et
                        /le dø   pasaʒe   œ̃ məsjø   e
une dame, ont été   blessés.
yn dam   ɔ̃   t‿ete blɛse/
(First bystander) The two passengers, a man and a woman, were injured.

(Le deuxième spectateur) On vient de les transporter à
/ lə døzjɛm   spɛktatœːr ɔ̃ vjɛ̃ d le trɑ̃spɔrte   a
l'hôpital.
l ɔpital/
(Second bystander) They've just been taken to the hospital.

---

[1] Imperfect indicative of **s'arrêter**, *to stop.*

(Le premier spectateur) Heureusement que personne n'a été
/œrøzmã k pɛrsɔn na ete

tué.
tye/

(First bystander) Luckily no one was killed.

La voiture doit être bien abîmée.
/la vwatyːr dwat‿ɛtr bjɛ̃‿abime/
The car must have been totaled.

(Le deuxième spectateur) Une roue avant est arrachée, le
/yn ru avã ɛ t araʃe lə

radiateur défoncé.
radjatœːr defɔ̃se/

*(Second bystander) A front wheel was ripped off, and the
radiator was smashed in.*

(Le premier spectateur) Ça, ce n'est rien. Moi, je suis
/sa s nɛ rjɛ̃ mwa ʒ sɥi

mécanicien. Je peux remettre tout ça à neuf.
mekanisjɛ̃ ʒə pø r(ə)mɛtr tu sa a nœf/

*(First bystander) That's no big deal. I'm a mechanic. I can
fix all that up like new.*

Je parie que c'est la même voiture qui nous a doublés à toute
/ʒə pari k sɛ la mɛm vwatyːr ki nuz‿a duble a tut

vitesse.
vitɛs/

I bet it's the same car that passed us at top speed.

Ça ne m'étonnerait pas.
/sa n metɔnrɛ pɑ/

I wouldn't be surprised.

Vous voyez, c'est toujours dangereux de faire de la vitesse.
/vu vwaje se tuʒuːr dãʒrø d fɛːr də la vitɛs/
You see, it's always dangerous to speed.

AUTOMOBILE

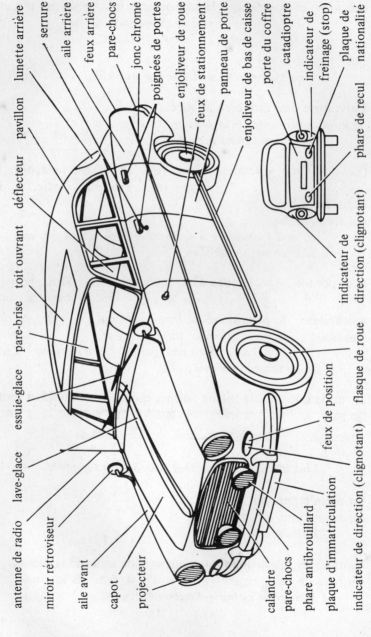

antenne de radio
miroir rétroviseur
aile avant
capot
projecteur
calandre
pare-chocs
phare antibrouillard
plaque d'immatriculation
indicateur de direction (clignotant)

lave-glace
essuie-glace
pare-brise
toit ouvrant
déflecteur
pavillon

feux de position
flasque de roue

lunette arrière
serrure
aile arrière
feux arrière
pare-chocs
jonc chromé
poignées de portes
enjoliveur de roue
feux de stationnement
panneau de porte

enjoliveur de bas de caisse
porte du coffre
catadioptre
indicateur de freinage (stop)
plaque de nationalité

indicateur de direction (clignotant)
phare de recul

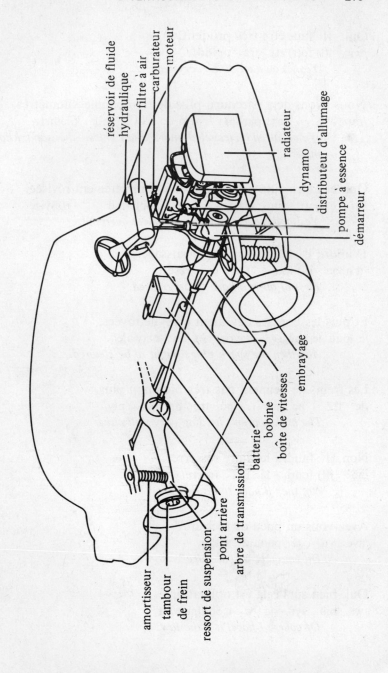

réservoir de fluide hydraulique
filtre à air
carburateur
moteur
radiateur
dynamo
distributeur d'allumage
pompe à essence
démarreur
embrayage
boîte de vitesses
bobine
batterie
arbre de transmission
pont arrière
ressort de suspension
tambour de frein
amortisseur

Oui. Il faut être très prudent.
/wi   i(l) fo(t) ɛtr trɛ prydɑ̃/
Yes. You have to be very careful.

Nous avons déjà parcouru plus de trente mille kilomètres.
/nuz‿avɔ̃   deʒa parkury ply də trɑ̃t   mil kilɔmɛtr/
*We've already traveled more than thirty thousand kilo-
meters.*

Oui, et notre auto a besoin d'être complètement revisée.
/wi e nɔtr oto a bəzwɛ̃ d ɛtr kɔ̃plɛtmɑ̃   r(ə)vize/
Yes, and our car needs a complete overhaul.

D'abord il   faudra faire un graissage.
/d abɔːr i(l) fodra   fɛr   ɑ̃̃ grɛsaːʒ/
First of all it'll have to be greased.

Et puis les bougies devraient être nettoyées.
/e pɥu le buʒi   dəvrɛ   t‿ɛtr nɛtwaje/
And then the spark plugs ought to be cleaned.

Les freins ne tiennent pas très bien non plus.
/le frɛ̃   nə tjɛn   pɑ trɛ bjɛ̃ nɔ̃   ply/
The brakes aren't holding very well either.

Non, il   faudra les faire resserrer.
/nɔ̃   i(l) fodra   le fɛːr rəsɛre/
No, they'll have to be tightened.

Avez-vous un pneu de secours?
/ave vu   ɑ̃̃ pnø d səkur/
Do you have a spare tire?

Oui, bien sûr! cela est obligatoire.
/wi bjɛ̃ syr sla ɛ t‿ɔbligatwaːr/
Of course I have! it's the law.

Attention! Pas par là. La rue est barrée.
/atɑ̃sjɔ̃   pɑ par la   la ry   ɛ   bare/
Look out! Not that way. The road's closed.

Zut! Et celle-là est à sens unique.
/zyt e sɛl   la ɛ t‿a sɑ̃s   ynik/
Drat! And the one over there is one-way.

Arrêtez. Je vais descendre acheter des cigarettes.
/arɛte   ʒ(ə) vɛ desɑ̃ːdr aʃte   de sigarɛt/
Stop. I'm going to get out and buy some cigarettes.

Je ne peux pas stationner ici. Il y a une bouche à incendie.
/ʒə n pø   pɑ stɑsjɔne   isi i(l) j a yn buʃ   a ɛ̃sɑ̃di/
I can't park here. There's a fire hydrant.

Alors, avancez un peu plus loin.
/alɔːr avɑ̃se   œ̃ pø ply lwɛ̃/
Then go on a bit farther.

Si j'attrape une contravention, ce sera de votre faute!
/si ʒatrap   yn kɔ̃travɑ̃sjɔ̃   sə sra d vɔtr   fot/
If I get a ticket, it'll be your fault!

REMARQUES

1. The following are words that may be confusing:
essence /ɛsɑ̃ːs/ f., *gas* (for a car, for example); **le gaz** /gaz/, (*natural*)
gas; **pétrole** /petrol/, *oil* (*petroleum*); **mazout** /mazut/, *heating oil*;
huile /ɥil/f., *oil—gasoline* or *cooking*.

2. Useful expressions: **donner de l'essence** /dɔne d(ə)
lɛsɑ̃ːs/, *to give it gas*; **huile lourde** (**moyenne, légère**) /ɥil lurd mwajɛn
leʒɛːr/, *heavy* (*medium, light*) *oil*; **fuir** (**avoir une fuite**) /fɥir avwaːr
yn fɥit/, *to leak*; **gonfler** /gɔ̃fle/, *to fill with air*; **dégonfler** /degɔ̃fle/,
to deflate; **baisser les phares** /bɛse le far/, *to dim the lights*; **le feu
pilote** /fø pilot/, *taillight*; **caler le moteur** /kale lə mɔtœːr/, *to shut off
the motor.*

3. Additional signs: **Danger** /dɑ̃ʒe/, *Danger*; **Ralentir** ralɑ̃tiːr/, *Slow*; **Tenez Votre Droite** /tɔne vɔtr(ə) drwat/,· *Keep Right*; **Tournant Dangereux** /turnɑ̃ dɑ̃ʒrø/, *Dangerous Curve*.

4. Some vocabulary suggested by **la vitesse** /vitɛs/, *speed*: **faire de la vitesse** /fɛːr də la vitɛs/, *to speed*; **indicateur de vitesse** /ɛ̃dikatœr də vitɛs/, *speedometer*.

5. Some parts of a car: **le pare-brise** /parbriz/, *windshield*; **un essuie-glace** /ɛsɥi glas/, *windshield wiper*; **un engrenage** /ɑ̃grənaʒ/, gear; **une courroie** /kurwa/, *belt*.

6. Some vocabulary for repairs: **roder les soupapes** /rɔde le supap/, *to grind the valves*; **le cric** /krik/, *jack*; **un accu (accumulateur)** /aky akymylatœːr/, *battery*; **un arbre de transmission** /arbr də trɑ̃smisjɔ̃/, *axle*; **un écrou** /ekru/, *nut*; **un outil** /uti/, *tool*; **le tournevis** /turnəvis/, *screwdriver*; **la vis** /vis/, *screw*.

Voyage en avion

An Airplane Trip

J'ai l'intention de faire un voyage au Maroc au printemps
/ʒe l ɛ̃tɑ̃sjɔ̃   d fɛr   œ̃ vwajaʒ o marɔk o prɛ̃tɑ̃
prochain. Y êtes-vous jamais allé?
prɔʃɛ̃   i ɛt vu   ʒamɛ z ale/
> *I plan on taking a trip to Morocco next spring. Have you
> ever been there?*

Mais oui, j'y suis allé le mois dernier en avion.
/mɛ wi   ʒ i sɥiz ale lə mwa dɛrnjɛr ɑ̃ n avjɔ̃/
> *Oh yes, I went last month by plane.*

Tiens! Et vous avez fait un bon voyage?
/tjɛ̃   e vuz ave fɛt œ̃ bɔ̃ vwajaːʒ/
> *Well! And did you have a nice trip?*

Superbe. Et c'est si pratique. Pensez donc! En trois heures
/sypɛrb   e sɛ   si pratik   pɑ̃se dɔ̃ːk   ɑ̃ trwaz œːr
de temps on arrive à Rabat.
də tɑ̃   ɔ̃ n ariv a raba/
> *First-rate. And it's so practical. Just think! In three hours'
> time you reach Rabat.*

Vous ne vous êtes pas senti mal à cause de l'altitude?
/vu   n vuz ɛt pɑ sɑ̃ti mal a koz   də l altityd/
> *Didn't you feel sick because of the altitude?*

Mais non. D'ailleurs on ne vole pas bien haut, sauf au-dessus
/mɛ nɔ̃ dajœːr   ɔ̃ n vɔl pɑ bjɛ̃ o   sof o dsy
des Pyrénées.
de pirene/

> *Oh, no. Anyway they don't fly very high, except over the*
> *Pyrenees.*

Moi, ça me fait toujours mal aux oreilles quand on dépasse
/mwa sa m fɛ tuzuːr   mal oz‿ɔrɛːj   kɑ̃   t‿ɔ̃ depɑs
trois mille mètres.
trwa mil mɛtr/

> *My ears always ache when I get above three thousand*
> *meters.*

Moi, pas du tout. L'altitude ne me gêne pas.
/mwa pɑ dy tu   laltityd   nə m ʒɛn pɑ/

> *Mine never do. The altitude doesn't bother me.*

Vous n'avez pas eu de tempête?
/vu nave paz‿y də tɑ̃pɛt/

> *You didn't have any storm?*

Non, le vol a été très calme, sauf au-dessus des Pyrénées, où
/nɔ̃ l(ə) vɔl a ete trɛ kalm   sof odsy   de pirene   u
il y avait quelques « poches d'air ».
i(l) j avɛ kɛlkə   pɔʃ   d ɛːr/

> *No, the flight was very calm, except above the Pyrenees*
> *where there were some air pockets.*

A combien de bagages a-t-on droit?
/a kɔ̃bjɛ̃   d bagaːʒ   a t ɔ̃ drwat/

> *How much is the baggage allowance?*

A vingt kilos, je crois.
/a vɛ̃   kilo ʒə krwa/

> *About twenty kilos, I think.*

Vous avez sans doute pris l'avion à l'aéroport de Roissy.
/vuz‿ave sã dut pri lavjɔ̃ a laeropɔːr də rwasi/
You probably took the plane at Roissy airport.

Oui.
/wi/
Yes.

Vous n'avez pas fait escale?
/vu nave pɑ fɛ(t) ɛskal/
You didn't make any stops?

Non, en Boeing on voyage sans escale de Paris à Rabat.
/nɔ̃ ã bɔiɲ ɔ̃ vwajaʒ sãz‿ɛskal də pari a raba/
No, in a 707 you fly direct from Paris to Rabat.

Ainsi vous avez survolé les Pyrénées et la Méditerranée?
/ɛ̃si vuz‿ave syrvɔle le pirene e la meditɛrane/
Then you flew over the Pyrenees and the Mediterranean?

C'est ça. Et nous avons atterri à Rabat sans le moindre
/sɛ sa e nuz‿avɔ̃ z‿atɛri a raba sã l(ə) mwɛ̃ːdr
incident.
ɛ̃sidã/
That's right. And we landed at Rabat with absolutely no problem (lit. " without the slightest mishap ").

REMARQUES

Additional vocabulary: **une aile** /ɛl/, *wing*; **décoller** /dekɔle/, *to take off*; **amérir** /ameriːr/, *to come down on water*; **un avion de bombardement** /avjɔ̃ d bɔ̃bardəmã/ ,*bomber*; **le hangar** /ãgaːr/, *hangar*; **le mécanicien** /mekanisjɛ̃/, *mechanic*; **le moteur** /mɔtœːr/, *engine*; **le parachute** /paraʃyt/, *parachute*; **le pilote** /pilɔt/, *pilot*; **j'ai fait une partie du trajet en avion** /ʒe fɛ(t) yn parti dy traʒɛ ãn avjɔ̃/, *I flew part of the way.*

6

Pour les jeunes

For Young People

Séjour dans une famille française

A Stay with a French Family

■ **Echanges**   *Exchange programs*

Through exchange programs families in France "exchange" teen-agers of the same age for an agreed length of time with similar families in other countries. The only cost involved is a round-trip ticket. Language courses are sometimes available.

For more information, contact the following organizations:

Comité d'Accueil des Elèves des Ecoles Publiques
7, rue Quentin Bauchart
75008 – Paris
Tél: 225-93-19
(Grande Bretagne, Allemagne, Espagne, Etats-Unis, Canada).

Bureau International de Liaison et de Documentation
50, rue Laborde
75008 – Paris
Tél: 387-25-50
(Allemagne).

Clubs des Quatre Vents
1, rue Gozlin
75006 – Paris
Tél: 033-70-25
(Grande-Bretagne, Allemagne, Espagne).

Echanges Internationaux entre Familles Chrétiennes
1, rue Gozlin
75006 – Paris
Tél: 033-92-11
(Grande-Bretagne, Irlande, Espagne, Allemagne, Etats-Unis).

Vacances Jeunes
67, rue de Rome
75008 – Paris
Tél: 292-29-29
(Grande-Bretagne, Allemagne, Espagne, Etats-Unis).

Amitié Internationale
123, rue de la Tour
75016 – Paris
Tél: 504-18-10
(Grande-Bretagne).

■ Hôte Payant   *Paying guest*

A stay as a paying guest in France allows you to perfect your knowledge of French and participate in family life. The stays must be of a minimum of fifteen days, and the cost varies. The French families are chosen by the following organizations:

Accueil Amical
21, rue St-Augustin
75002 – Paris
Tél: 742-29-12
Jeunes de 12 à 25 ans. Toute l'année dans des familles parisiennes.

Centre de Tourisme Universitaire
64, boulevard de Courcelles
75017 – Paris
Tél: 227-67-34
Pour les étudiants américains.

Amitié Mondiale
39, rue Cambon
75001 – Paris
Tél: 702-26-21
Jeunes de 15 à 25 ans. Toute l'année à Paris et en province.

Club des Quatre Vents
1, rue Gozlin
75005 – Paris
Tél: 033-70-25
Séjour durant l'été à Paris et en province.

Centre des Echanges Internationaux de la Moselle
40, rue St-Marcel
57000 – Metz
Tél: 68-84-18

Ligue d'Amitié Internationale
c/o Mme Libot
54, boulevard de Vaugirard
75015 – Paris
Tél: 734-96-29 (8h à 9h).

Centre de Rencontres Internationales de Dijon
1, boulevard Champollion
21000 – Dijon
Tél: 32-39-08

Relations Internationales
100, rue St-Lazare
75009 – Paris
Tél: 874-93-65
Jeunes de 15 à 25 ans. Toute l'année à Paris et en province.

Auto–stop

Hitchhiking

Hitchhiking in France has the same risks and insurance problems as in America—and the same advantages. However, it is more difficult to get a ride in France, and almost impossible in the city/in a group (more than two people)/or carrying a lot of luggage.

It is possible in certain cities to contact drivers who are willing to take a rider as long as he shares the gas expenses. The following organizations can be contacted for this purpose:

Provoya
14, rue du Fg St-Denis
75010 – Paris
Tél: 770-28-59,   770-64-13,
770-36-31,   523-36-31,   523-
27-99

Allauto
67, rue Colbert
59000 – Lille
Tél: 54-15-27

S.O.S. Départ
2, place Jacquin Gasquet
13100 – Aix-en-Provence
Tél: 27-52-18

S.O.S. Départ
rue Loubon
13003 – Marseille
Tél: 62-70-46

Téléstop
1, place des Hauts Murats
31000 – Toulouse
Tél: 52-21-37

Auto-Contact
6, rue J.B. Poquelin-Molière
33000 – Bordeaux
Tél: 44-33-68

Hôtels bon marché

Inexpensive Hotels

75001 - Paris

Hôtel Richelieu Nazarin
51, rue de Richelieu
Tél: 742-48-13
Métro: Palais-Royal

Hôtel du Jura
66, rue de l'Arbre Sec
Tél: 236-92-50
Métro: Louvre

75002 - Paris

Hôtel du Caire
46, rue du Caire
Tél: 508-05-85
Métro: Bonne Nouvelle

Hôtel Moderne
100, rue d'Aboukir
Tél: 236-91-16
Métro: Sentier

Hôtel Angleterre
56, rue Montmartre
Tél: 236-93-71
Métro: Halles-Sentier

75004 - Paris

Sully Hôtel
48, rue Saint Antoine
Tél: 272-49-32
Métro: Bastille

75005 - Paris

Hôtel du Progrès
50, rue Gay Lussac
Tél: 033-53-18
Métro: Luxembourg

Modern Hôtel
5, rue de Broca
Tél: 331-23-29
Métro: Censier-Daubenton

Résidence de Lutèce
59, rue du Cardinal Lemoine
Tél: 033-73-86
Métro: Odéon

Hôtel Saint-Michel
19, rue Cujas
Tél: 033-47-98
Métro: Luxembourg

75009 - Paris

Hôtel le Brittany
3, rue Saint Lazare
Tél: 878-44-50
Métro: N. Dame de Lorette

75011 - Paris

Hôtel Amya
5, Passage Vialet
Tél: 700-05-41
Métro: Voltaire

Hôtel Saint-Bernard
44, rue St-Bernard
Tél: 805-99-97
Métro: Ledru-Rollin

75014 - Paris

Hôtel Orléans Châtillon
108, avenue du Général Leclerc
Tél: 250-07-00
Métro: Alésia

75015 - Paris

Hôtel Star
87, avenue Emile Zola
Tél: 578-08-22
Métro: Javel

Hôtel Garibaldi
92, boulevard Garibaldi
Tél: 783-22-79
Métro: La Motte Piquet
   Grenelle

75017 - Paris

Hôtel des Batignolles
36, rue des Batignolles
Tél: 387-76-07
Métro: Clichy

Grand Hôtel Métropolitain
22, rue Boursault
Tél: 522-45-34
Métro: Rome

75020 - Paris

Hôtel de l'Union
65, rue des Pyrénées
Tél: 805-57-72
Métro: Maraicher

BANLIEUE

94410 - Saint-Maurice

Hôtel Sélect Saint Maurice
41, rue Adrien d'Amalix
Tél: 368-20-03

91410 - Dourdan

Hôtel Dourdan
1, rue de Bonniveau
Tél: 492-76-15

92400 - Courbevoie

Hôtel de Blois
85, boulevard Saint-Denis
Métro: Porte Champeret
Tél: 333-13-35
(bus: 163 ou 164).

Restaurants bon marché

Inexpensive Restaurants

75001 - Paris
Bistrot des Halles
7, rue du Roule
Tél: 231-33-20
Fermé le dimanche.

L'Ecuelle
28, rue de l'Arbre-Sec
Tél: 231-97-82
Fermé le dimanche.

Le Vieil Ecu
166, rue Saint Honoré
Tél: 231-03-24
Fermé le dimanche.

75002 - Paris
Brouillet
5, rue Paul Lelong
Tél: 236-26-08
Ouvert de 11h à 14h30
Fermé le soir.

75003 - Paris
Aux Routiers
29, rue Beaubourg
Tél: 887-95-18
Fermé le dimanche

75004 - Paris
Le Monde des Chimères
69, rue Saint-Louis-en-l'Ile
Tél: 033-45-27
Fermé le dimanche

Le Trumilou
84, quai de l'Hôtel de Ville
Tél: 277-63-98
Fermé le lundi

75005 - Paris
Chez Paulette
28, rue des Bernardins
Tél: 033-63-84
Fermé le dimanche

75006 - Paris
Restaurant des Arts
73, rue de Seine
Tél: 326-11-79
Fermé le samedi et le dimanche

75007 - Paris
La Cigale
11 bis, rue Chomel
Tél: 548-67-87
Fermé le dimanche.

L'Escale Bleue
196, rue de Grenelle
Tél: 551-40-32
Fermé le dimanche

75008 - Paris

Boutique à Sandwichs
12, rue du Colisée
Tél: 359-34-32
Fermé le dimanche

Le Chambiges
4, rue de Chambiges
Tél: 359-45-32
Fermé le dimanche

Le Cloyères
9, rue Laborde
Tél: 387-93-26
Déjeuner seulement

Valentin
19, rue Marbeuf
Tél: 359-80-11
Fermé le dimanche

75009 - Paris

L'Ancien Chartier
7, rue du Faubourg Montmartre
Tél: 770-86-29

La Boule Rouge
1, rue de la Boule Rouge
Tél: 770-43-90
Fermé le dimanche

75010 - Paris

Bar du Combat Roggero
37, avenue Claude Vellefaux
Tél: 205-30-01
Fermé le dimanche

Julien
16, Faubourg Saint Denis
Tél: 770-12-06
Fermé le dimanche

75011 - Paris

Chez Georges
1, rue du Chemin Vert
Tél: 805-01-30

Munchner Pschorrbrau Haus
14, place de la Bastille
Tél: 343-42-76
Service jusqu'à 23h.

75012 - Paris

Au Béarnais
270, rue du Faubourg St-Antoine
Tél: 307-73-62
Fermé le mercredi

Le Petit Pot
180, rue du Faubourg Saint-Antoine
Tél: 343-91-13
Fermé le lundi

75013 - Paris

L'Arago
13, boulevard Arago
Tél: 707-79-07
Fermé le mercredi soir et jeudi

75014 - Paris

Desperbasque
140, rue de la Tombe Issoire
Tél: 331-29-79
Fermé le dimanche.

Les Mille Colonnes
20 bis, rue de la Gaité
Tél: 326-68-69

Au Petit Bar
7, rue Campagne Première
Tél: 326-93-04
Fermé le dimanche

75015 - Paris

Au Beaujolais
17, rue de Lourmel
Tél: 783-31-63
Fermé le dimanche

75016 - Paris

La Chope Galilée
36, rue Hamelin
et 14, rue Galilée
Tél: 727-90-66
Fermé le samedi soir et le
     dimanche.

75017 - Paris

Le Relais Saint-Hubert
117, rue des Dames
Tél: 387-63-08
Fermé le dimanche

75018 - Paris

Chez Ginette
101, rue Caulaincourt
Tél: 606-01-49
Fermé le dimanche

Les Négociants
27, rue Lambert
Tél: 606-15-11
Tous les jours, sauf dimanche

75019 - Paris

La Biche Egarée
66, avenue Jean Jaurès
Tél: 208-84-77
Fermé le dimanche.

L'Etape
351, rue des Pyrénées
Tél: 636-19-45
Fermé le lundi

Relais Villette
25, avenue Corentin Cariou
Tél: 607-91-17
Fermé le dimanche

75020 - Paris

Le Don Quichotte
127, rue de Ménilmontant

APPENDIX

1. Gender

   Nouns are either masculine or feminine. Nouns denoting male beings are masculine. Nouns denoting female beings are feminine. The gender of other nouns must be learned by usage.

2. The Definite Article *the*

	SINGULAR		PLURAL
Masc.	**le**		**les**
Fem.	**la**		**les**

le timbre	the stamp	**les timbres**	the stamps
l'avion	the plane	**les avions**	the planes
la cigarette	the cigarette	**les cigarettes**	the cigarettes
l'heure	the hour	**les heures**	the hours

   Le and **la** become **l'** before a vowel or mute **h.**

   Contraction

   de + le = du of (from) the   **à + le = au** to (at, in) the
   de + les = des of (from) the   **à + les = aux** to (at, in) the
   de + la and **de + l'**, **à + la** and **à + l'** do not contract.

le plan du bateau	**Je vais au cinéma.**
the plan of the boat	I am going to the " movies."
la visite des passeports	**Il parle aux employés.**
the passport inspection	He speaks to the employees.

The definite article is used

a) With nouns denoting all of a class:

Les femmes aiment les bijoux.   Women like jewels.

b) With abstract nouns:

Le courage est nécessaire.   Courage is necessary.

c) With adjectives denoting a language:

L'anglais est difficile.   English is difficult.

Except after **parler** and **en:**

Il parle français et je traduis en anglais.   He speaks French and I translate into English.

d) With geographical names (**la France, l'Angleterre, le Canada, l'Amérique,** etc.) except after **en:**

La France est un beau pays.   France is a beautiful country.
Il va au Canada.   He is going to Canada.
Je vais en France.   I am going to France.

Geographical names ending in silent **e** are usually feminine; others are masculine. Exception: **le Mexique,** *Mexico.*

e) With a title not in direct address, except with **monsieur, madame, mademoiselle:**

Le général Leblanc est ici.   General White is here.
Monsieur Lenoir est à Paris.   Mr. Black is in Paris.

f) With nouns of weight and measure:

Cela coûte vingt francs le mètre.   That costs twenty francs a meter.

g) Instead of possessive adjectives with parts of the body:

Que tenez-vous à la main?   What are you holding in your hand?

h) With names of seasons, expressions of time, meals, etc:.

Le printemps est arrivé.   Spring has come.
Le dîner est à huit heures.   Dinner is at eight.

i) With **de** to indicate a partitive noun:

Avez-vous du pain?   Have you (some) bread?
J'ai de l'argent.   I have (some) money.
J'ai de l'encre.   I have (some) ink.
Il a des timbres.   He has (some) stamps.

Except: 1) in a negation; 2) when an adjective precedes the noun; 3) after an expression of quantity:

Je n'ai pas de timbres.   I have no stamps.
Elle a de grands yeux.   She has big eyes.
J'ai assez d'argent.   I have enough money.

3. The Indefinite Article *a, an*

	SINGULAR		PLURAL	
Masc.	**un**	a (one)	**des**	some
Fem.	**une**	a (one)	**des**	some

Donnez-moi un timbre.   Give me a stamp.
Donnez-moi des timbres.   Give me some stamps.

4. The indefinite article is omitted

a) Before unmodified nouns indicating nationality or profession:

Je suis Français.   I am a Frenchman.
Il est aviateur.   He is an aviator.

b) Before **cent** and **mille**:

J'ai cent (mille) francs.   I have a hundred (a thousand) francs.

5. Plural of Nouns

a) Nouns regularly form their plural by adding **s** to the singular. If the singular ends in **s**, there is no change.

le timbre	the stamp	**les timbres**	the stamps
le fils	the son	**les fils**	the sons

b) Nouns ending in **au** or **eu** take **x** instead of **s,** and names ending in **al** change to **aux**:

le chapeau	the hat	**les chapeaux**	the hats
le cheval	the horse	**les chevaux**	the horses

6. Adjectives agree in gender and number with the nouns they modify.

a) The feminine of most adjectives is formed by adding **e** to the masculine:

un grand pays   a large country
une grande ville   a large city

b) Adjectives ending in **e** are invariable in the singular:

un homme riche   a rich man
une femme riche   a rich woman

c) There are some exceptional feminine endings, such as:

bon, bonne	good	**beau, belle**	beautiful
blanc, blanche	white	**doux, douce**	sweet

7. Position of Adjectives
Adjectives may precede or follow the noun. A few generally precede: **petit, grand, beau,** etc.

A few generally follow: adjectives of nationality and of color:

une petite maison   a little house
une robe bleue   a blue gown
un livre français   a French book

8. Comparison
Place **plus,** *more,* **moins,** *less,* **aussi,** *as,* **si,** *so,* before the adjective or adverb; and **que,** *than, as,* after it:

Pierre est plus grand que Paul.   Peter is taller than Paul.
Paul parle moins bien que Pierre.   Paul speaks less well than Peter.

Henri est aussi grand qu'Albert. Henry is as tall as Albert.

Georges n'est pas si grand que vous. George is not so tall as you.

In the superlative, place the definite article or possessive adjective before **plus** or **moins:**

le plus beau jardin the most beautiful garden
la plus grande maison the largest house
le plus souvent most often

Irregular Comparisons

bon	good	**meilleur**	better	**le meilleur**	the best
bien	well	**mieux**	better	**le mieux**	the best
peu	little	**moins**	less	**le moins**	the least

9. Possessive Adjectives

	SINGULAR		PLURAL
	Masc.	*Fem.*	*Masc. and Fem.*
my	**mon**	**ma**	**mes**
thy	**ton**	**ta**	**tes**
his ⎫			
her ⎬	**son**	**sa**	**ses**
its ⎭			
our	**notre**	**notre**	**nos**
your	**votre**	**votre**	**vos**
their	**leur**	**leur**	**leurs**

10. The possessive adjective agrees with the noun that comes immediately after it, and it must be repeated before each noun:

mon père et ma mère my father and mother
Victor et sa sœur Victor and his sister
Hélène et son frère Helen and her brother
vos parents et leurs enfants your parents and their children

Mon, ton, son are used instead of **ma, ta, sa** before feminine singular nouns beginning with a vowel or mute **h:**

mon amie my lady friend

11. Possessive Pronouns

	SINGULAR		PLURAL	
	Masc.	*Fem.*	*Masc.*	*Fem.*
mine	le mien	la mienne	les miens	les miennes
yours (thine)	le tien	la tienne	les tiens	les tiennes
his hers its	le sien	la sienne	les siens	les siennes
ours	le nôtre	la nôtre	les nôtres	
yours	le vôtre	la vôtre	les vôtres	
theirs	le leur	la leur	les leurs	

12. The possessive pronouns, like possessive adjectives, agree in gender and number with the object possessed:

> **votre chambre et la mienne**   your room and mine
> **mon hôtel et le sien**   my hotel and his

13. Distinction of ownership is expressed by the use of the possessive pronoun. Mere ownership is expressed by **être + à:**

> **A qui sont ces mouchoirs?**   Whose handkerchiefs are these?
> **Ils ne sont pas à moi.**   They are not mine.
> **Les miens sont bleus.**   Mine are blue.

14. Demonstrative Adjectives

> *this* or *that* = **ce** before a masculine noun beginning with a consonant
> **cet** before a masculine noun beginning with a vowel or a mute **h**
> **cette** before a feminine noun
> *these* or *those* = **ces** before any plural noun

There is no special word in French to distinguish between *this* and *that*, nor between *these* and *those*. When such distinction is necessary, **-ci** *here*, or **-là,** *there*, is added to the noun:

> **Cet homme-ci est plus riche que cet homme-là.**   This man is wealthier than that man.

15. Demonstrative Pronouns

Masc. Sing.	**celui**	⎫ this, that, the one
Fem. Sing.	**celle**	⎭
Masc. Pl.	**ceux**	⎫ these, those, the ones
Fem. Pl.	**celles**	⎭

When the demonstrative pronoun is not followed by a relative pronoun or by an adjective phrase, **-ci** or **-là** must be affixed:

> **Regardez ces deux tableaux.** Look at those two pictures.
> **Celui-ci est plus beau que celui-là.** This one is more beautiful than that one.
> **Voici celui que je préfère.** Here is the one I prefer.

16. Adverbs are usually formed by adding **–ment** to the feminine singular of the adjective:

> **parfait, –e** perfect   **parfaitement** perfectly
> EXCEPTIONS: **bien** well   **mal** badly   **vite** quickly

17. Negatives

> **ne . . . pas** not   **ne . . . que** only
> **ne . . . rien** nothing   **ne . . . plus** no more (longer)
> **ne . . . jamais** never   **ne . . . personne** nobody

a) The verb comes between **ne** and the negative word:

> **Je comprends.** I understand.
> **Je ne comprends pas.** I do not understand.

b) If the negative word is subject of the verb, it precedes **ne**:

> **Personne ne comprend.** Nobody understands.

18. Personal Pronouns

SUBJECT	DIRECT OBJECT	INDIRECT OBJECT	REFLEXIVE	DISJUNCTIVE
je I	**me** me	**me** (to) me	**me** myself	**moi** me (I)
tu you (*fam.*)	**te** you	**te** (to) you	**te** yourself	**toi** you
il he, it	**le** him, it	**lui** to him, to her, to it	**se** himself, herself, itself	**lui** him (he), it **elle** her (she), it
elle she, it	**la** her, it			
nous we	**nous** us	**nous** (to) us	**nous** ourselves	**nous** us
vous you	**vous** you	**vous** (to) you	**vous** yourselves	**vous** you
ils **elles** } they	**les** them	**leur** (to) them	**se** themselves	**eux** **elles** } them

19. Position of Personal Pronouns

a) Object pronouns are placed before the verb:

Je le vois.   I see him.
Je ne le vois pas.   I do not see him.

b) Object pronouns follow affirmative commands but precede negative commands:

Donnez-le-moi.   Give it to me.
Ne me le donnez pas.   Don't give it to me.

c) When there are two object pronouns, the indirect precedes the direct, except when both are in the third person:

Il me le donne.   He gives it to me.
Je le lui donne.   I give it to him (her).

20. The pronoun **en** is used in reference to things

a) To replace a noun or a clause preceded by **de**:

Il aime son pays. Il en parle souvent.   He loves his country. He speaks of it often.

b) To replace a partitive:

Combien de timbres avez-vous? J'en ai deux.   How many stamps have you? I have two (of them).

21. The pronoun and adverb **y** refers to things or places preceded by **à, dans, sur, chez,** etc.

il y a   there is, there are
Je vais à Paris. J'y vais.   (I am going there.)
Il va chez sa mère. Il y va.   (He is going there.)

22. The disjunctive forms are used

a) When the personal pronoun stands alone:

Qui est là? — Moi.   Who is there? I.

b) After a preposition:

Je vais avec eux.   I am going with them.

23. Interrogation

a) The words **est-ce que** may always be used to introduce a question without changing the word order:

Est-ce que vous parlez français? Do you speak French?
Est-ce que votre ami est jeune? Is your friend young?

b) When the subject of the verb is a pronoun, the subject may be placed after the verb:

Vous parlez français
Parlez-vous français } Do you speak French?

c) When the subject is a noun, the noun stands before the verb and a corresponding pronoun is placed after the verb:

Votre ami est-il jeune? Is your friend young?

d) –t– is added for euphony when a third-person verb ends in a vowel and the following pronoun-subject begins with a vowel:

Y a-t-il un remède? Is there a cure for it?

24. Relative Pronouns

a) **qui** who, which (*subject*)
   que whom, which (*direct object*)
   dont of whom, of which

l'homme qui parle the man who is speaking
les dames que vous voyez the ladies (whom) you see
le pays dont je parle the country of which I speak

b) **Lequel,** in its appropriate form, is used after prepositions in reference to things:

les plumes avec lesquelles j'écris the pens with which I write

c) **ce qui, ce que** = *that which, what*

Faites ce qui est juste. Do what (that which) is right.

25. Interrogative Adjectives and Pronouns

    a) Adjectives

	SINGULAR		PLURAL	
Masc.	**quel**	} what? which?	**quels**	} what? which?
Fem.	**quelle**		**quelles**	

    Quel livre aimez-vous?   Which book do you like?
    Quelles sont vos raisons?   What are your reasons?

    Quel is also used in exclamations:

    quelle belle femme!   what (a) beautiful woman!

    b) Pronouns

    Referring to persons } **qui** *or* **qui est-ce qui?**   who?
                                 qui *or* **qui est-ce que?**   whom?

    Referring } **qu'est-ce qui?**   what? (*subject*)
    to things } **que** *or* **qu'est-ce que?**   what? (*direct object*)
                        quoi?   what? (*after preposition*)

    Qui est là?   Who is there?
    Qu'est-ce qui est arrivé?   What happened?
    Que faites-vous?   What are you doing?
    De quoi parlez-vous?   What are you speaking of?

26. Tenses of the Verb (that differ from English)

    a) The present indicative is often used for a future to indicate definite or immediate action:

    Je pars demain.   I (shall) leave tomorrow.

    The present indicative is used to indicate an action begun in the past and still going on:

    Il est malade depuis deux jours.   He has been ill for two days.

    b) The imperfect indicative is used to describe a state or condition, a continued or customary act:

    Il écrivait quand je suis entré.   He was writing when I entered.
    A Paris je dînais à huit heures.   In Paris I used to dine at eight o'clock.

c) The perfect indicative expresses completed action in the past:

Hier j'ai dîné à huit heures.   Yesterday I dined at eight o'clock.

d) The future is used when future time is implied after **quand, lorsque,** *when;* **dès que, aussitôt que,** *as soon as:*

Je le verrai quand il arrivera.   I'll see him when he arrives

27. The subjunctive is used principally

a) When the main clause expresses volition, emotion, doubt, etc.:

Il veut que je fasse cela.   He wants me to do that.
Je crains qu'il soit malade.   I am afraid he is ill.

b) After certain impersonal expressions, such as **il faut, il est nécessaire, il est possible,** etc.:

Il faut que j'y aille.   I must go there.
BUT: **Il est certain que j'y irai.**   It is certain that I'll go there.

c) After certain locutions such as **afin que, pour que,** *so that, in order that;* **à moins que,** *unless;* **avant que,** *before;* **bien que,** *although, even though:*

Je partirai bien qu'il fasse mauvais temps.   I shall leave even though the weather is bad.

d) In a relative clause that refers to an indefinite or negative antecedent:

Nous cherchons quelqu'un qui puisse se charger de la correspondance.   We are looking for someone who can take care of our correspondence.
Je ne connais personne qui sache le russe.   I don't know anybody who knows Russian.

28. When the main verb and the subordinate verb have the same subject, the infinitive is generally used instead of a subjunctive clause:

    Je regrette d'être en retard.   I am sorry I am late.

29. The infinitive is used instead of the English present participle

  a) After a preposition, except **en:**

    Il est parti sans me voir.   He left without seeing me.

  b) After **voir, entendre,** etc.:

    Je l'ai vu venir.   I saw him coming.
    Entendez-vous chanter?   Do you hear singing?

30. *a*) The true passive voice is formed with the verb **être** and the past participle, the agent being usually expressed by **par:**

    Il a été guéri par ce médecin.   He was cured by this doctor.

  b) In conversation the true passive is frequently replaced by the active form with **on** as subject when the agent is not expressed:

    Ici on parle anglais.   English is spoken here.
    On a arrêté le voleur.   The thief was caught.

  c) If the subject is a thing or an idea, the verb is often reflexive:

    Le livre se vend ici.   The book is sold here.
    Cela se comprend.   That is understood.

31. A few place names and their derivative adjectives. (The English equivalent is omitted when the meaning is apparent.)

Algérie *f.*	algérien, –ne
Allemagne *f.* (*Germany*)	allemand, –e (*German*)
Angleterre *f.*	anglais, –e

Argentine *f.*	argentin, –e
Autriche *f.*	auritchien, –ne
Belgique *f.*	belge
Brésil *m.*	brésilien, –ne
Canada *m.*	canadien, –ne
Chili *m.*	chilien, –ne
Chine *f.*	chinois, –e
Écosse *f.*	écossais, –e
Égypte *f.*	égyptien, –ne
Espagne *f.*	espagnol, –e
Europe *f.*	européen, –ne
France *f.*	français, –e
Grèce *f.*	grec, grecque
Hollande *f.*	hollandais, –e
Irlande *f.*	irlandais, –e
Italie *f.*	italien, –ne
Japon *m.*	japonais, –e
Maroc *m.*	marocain, –e
Mexique *m.*	mexicain, –e
Norvège *f.*	norvégien, –ne
Pérou *m.*	péruvien, –ne
Pologne *f.*	polonais, –e
Portugal *m.*	portugais, –e
Roumanie *f.*	roumain, –e
Russie *f.*	russe
Suède *f.*	suédois, –e
Suisse *f.*	suisse
Tchécoslovaquie *f.*	tchécoslovaque
Turquie *f.*	turc, turcque
Yougoslavie *f.*	yougoslave

32. Conjugation of the Verbs avoir and être

avoir *to have*   **être** *to be*

INDICATIVE MOOD

PRESENT

I have, am having, do have, etc.	*I am, am being, etc.*
j'ai	je suis
tu as	tu es
il a	il est

nous avons
vous avez
ils ont

nous sommes
vous êtes
ils sont

IMPERFECT

I was having, used to have, had, etc.   I was being, used to be, was, etc.

j'avais
tu avais
il avait

j'étais
tu étais
il était

nous avions
vous aviez
ils avaient

nous étions
vous étiez
ils étaient

PAST DEFINITE

I had, etc.

j'eus
tu eus
il eut

I was, etc.

je fus
tu fus
il fut

nous eûmes
vous eûtes
ils eurent

nous fûmes
vous fûtes
ils furent

PAST INDEFINITE

I have had, had, did have etc.

j'ai eu
tu as eu
il a eu

I have been, was, etc.

j'ai été
tu as été
il a été

nous avons eu
vous avez eu
ils ont eu

nous avons été
vous avez été
ils ont été

PLUPERFECT

I had had, etc.

j'avais eu
tu avais eu
il avait eu

I had been, etc.

j'avais été
tu avais été
il avait été

nous avions eu
vous aviez eu
ils avaient eu

nous avions été
vous aviez été
ils avaient été

Past Anterior

I had had, etc.	*I had been, etc.*
j'eus eu	j'eus été
tu eus eu	tu eus été
il eut eu	il eut été
nous eûmes eu	nous eûmes été
vous eûtes eu	vous eûtes été
ils eurent eu	ils eurent été

Future

I shall have, etc.	*I shall be, etc.*
j'aurai	je serai
tu auras	tu seras
il aura	il sera
nous aurons	nous serons
vous aurez	vous serez
ils auront	ils seront

Conditional

I should have, etc.	*I should be, etc.*
j'aurais	je serais
tu aurais	tu serais
il aurait	il serait
nous aurions	nous serions
vous auriez	vous seriez
ils auraient	ils seraient

Future Perfect

I shall have had, etc.	*I shall have been, etc.*
j'aurai eu	j'aurai été
tu auras eu	tu auras été
il aura eu	il aura été
nous aurons eu	nous aurons été
vous aurez eu	vous aurez été
ils auront eu	ils auront été

CONDITIONAL PERFECT

I should have had, etc.	*I should have been, etc.*
j'aurais eu	j'aurais été
tu aurais eu	tu aurais été
il aurait eu	il aurait été
nous aurions eu	nous aurions été
vous auriez eu	vous auriez été
ils auraient eu	ils auraient été

SUBJUNCTIVE MOOD

PRESENT

that I (may) have, etc.	*that I (may) be, etc.*
que j'aie	que je sois
que tu aies	que tu sois
qu'il ait	qu'il soit
que nous ayons	que nous soyons
que vous ayez	que vous soyez
qu'ils aient	qu'ils soient

IMPERFECT

that I might have, etc.	*that I might be, etc.*
que j'eusse	que je fusse
que tu eusses	que tu fusses
qu'il eût	qu'il fût
que nous eussions	que nous fussions
que vous eussiez	que vous fussiez
qu'ils eussent	qu'ils fussent

PERFECT

that I (may) have had, etc.	*that I (may) have been, etc.*
que j'aie eu	que j'aie été
que tu aies eu	que tu aies été
qu'il ait eu	qu'il ait été
que nous ayons eu	que nous ayons été
que vous ayez eu	que vous ayez été
qu'ils aient eu	qu'ils aient été

PLUPERFECT

that I might have had, etc.	*that I might have been, etc.*
que j'eusse eu	que j'eusse été
que tu eusses eu	que tu eusses été
qu'il eût eu	qu'il eût été
que nous eussions eu	que nous eussions été
que vous eussiez eu	que vous eussiez été
qu'ils eussent eu	qu'ils eussent été

IMPERATIVE

—	ayons, *let us have*	—	soyons, *let us be*
aie, *have* (*thou*)	ayez, *have* (*you*)	sois, *be* (*thou*)	soyez, *be* (*you*)

33. Regular Verbs: three conjugations

I	II	III

INFINITIVE

parler *to speak*	**finir** *to finish*	**entendre** *to hear*

PRESENT PARTICIPLE

parlant, *speaking*	finissant, *finishing*	entendant, *hearing*

PAST PARTICIPLE

parlé, *spoken*	fini, *finished*	entendu, *heard*

INDICATIVE MOOD

PRESENT

I speak, am speaking, etc.	*I finish, am finishing, etc.*	*I hear, am hearing, etc.*
je parle	je finis	j'entends
tu parles	tu finis	tu entends
il parle	il finit	il entend
nous parlons	nous finissons	nous entendons
vous parlez	vous finissez	vous entendez
ils parlent	ils finissent	ils entendent

IMPERFECT

I was speaking,
used to speak, etc.
je parlais
tu parlais
il parlait

nous parlions
vous parliez
ils parlaient

I was finishing,
used to finish, etc.
je finissais
tu finissais
il finissait

nous finissions
vous finissiez
ils finissaient

I was hearing, used
to hear, etc.
j'entendais
tu entendais
il entendait

nous entendions
vous entendiez
ils entendaient

PAST DEFINITE

I spoke, etc.
je parlai
tu parlas
il parla

nous parlâmes
vous parlâtes
ils parlèrent

I finished, etc.
je finis
tu finis
il finit

nous finîmes
vous finîtes
ils finirent

I heard, etc.
j'entendis
tu entendis
il entendit

nous entendîmes
vous entendîtes
ils entendirent

PAST INDEFINITE

I spoke, have
spoken, etc.
j'ai parlé
tu as parlé
il a parlé

nous avons parlé
vous avez parlé
ils ont parlé

I finished, have
finished, etc.
j'ai fini
tu as fini
il a fini

nous avons fini
vous avez fini
ils ont fini

I heard, have
heard, etc.
j'ai entendu
tu as entendu
il a entendu

nous avons entendu
vous avez entendu
ils ont entendu

PLUPERFECT

I had spoken, etc.
j'avais parlé
tu avais parlé
il avait parlé

nous avions parlé
vous aviez parlé
ils avaient parlé

I had finished, etc.
j'avais fini
tu avais fini
il avait fini

nous avions fini
vous aviez fini
ils avaient fini

I had heard, etc.
j'avais entendu
tu avais entendu
il avait entendu

nous avions entendu
vous aviez entendu
ils avaient entendu

Past Anterior

I had spoken, etc.	*I had finished, etc.*	*I had heard, etc.*
j'eus parlé	j'eus fini	j'eus entendu
tu eus parlé	tu eus fini	tu eus entendu
il eut parlé	il eut fini	il eut entendu
nous eûmes parlé	nous eûmes fini	nous eûmes entendu
vous eûtes parlé	vous eûtes fini	vous eûtes entendu
ils eurent parlé	ils eurent fini	ils eurent entendu

Future

I shall speak, etc.	*I shall finish, etc.*	*I shall hear, etc.*
je parlerai	je finirai	j'entendrai
tu parleras	tu finiras	tu entendras
il parlera	il finira	il entendra
nous parlerons	nous finirons	nous entendrons
vous parlerez	vous finirez	vous entendrez
ils parleront	ils finiront	ils entendront

Conditional

I should speak, etc.	*I should finish, etc.*	*I should hear, etc.*
je parlerais	je finirais	j'entendrais
tu parlerais	tu finirais	tu entendrais
il parlerait	il finirait	il entendrait
nous parlerions	nous finirions	nous entendrions
vous parleriez	vous finiriez	vous entendriez
ils parleraient	ils finiraient	ils entendraient

Future Perfect

I shall have spoken, etc.	*I shall have finished, etc.*	*I shall have heard, etc.*
j'aurai parlé	j'aurai fini	j'aurai entendu
tu auras parlé	tu auras fini	tu auras entendu
il aura parlé	il aura fini	il aura entendu
nous aurons parlé	nous aurons fini	nous aurons entendu
vous aurez parlé	vous aurez fini	vous aurez entendu
ils auront parlé	ils auront fini	ils auront entendu

CONDITIONAL PERFECT

I should have spoken, etc.	*I should have finished, etc.*	*I should have heard, etc.*
j'aurais parlé	j'aurais fini	j'aurais entendu
tu aurais parlé	tu aurais fini	tu aurais entendu
il aurait parlé	il aurait fini	il aurait entendu
nous aurions parlé	nous aurions fini	nous aurions entendu
vous auriez parlé	vous auriez fini	vous auriez entendu
ils auraient parlé	ils auraient fini	ils auraient entendu

SUBJUNCTIVE MOOD

PRESENT

that I (may) speak, etc.	*that I (may) finish, etc.*	*that I (may) hear, etc.*
que je parle	que je finisse	que j'entende
que tu parles	que tu finisses	que tu entendes
qu'il parle	qu'il finisse	qu'il entende
que nous parlions	que nous finissions	que nous entendions
que vous parliez	que vous finissiez	que vous entendiez
qu'ils parlent	qu'ils finissent	qu'ils entendent

IMPERFECT

that I (might) speak, etc.	*that I might) finish, etc.*	*that I (might) hear, etc.*
que je parlasse	que je finisse	que j'entendisse
que tu parlasses	que tu finisses	que tu entendisses
qu'il parlât	qu'il finît	qu'il entendît
que nous parlassions	que nous finissions	que nous entendissions
que vous parlassiez	que vous finissiez	que vous entendissiez
qu'ils parlassent	qu'ils finissent	qu'ils entendissent

PERFECT

that I (may) have spoken, etc.	*that I (may) have finished, etc.*	*that I (may) have heard, etc.*
que j'aie parlé	que j'aie fini	que j'aie entendu
que tu aies parlé	que tu aies fini	que tu aies entendu
qu'il ait parlé	qu'il ait fini	qu'il ait entendu

que nous ayons parlé que nous ayons fini que nous ayons entendu
que vous ayez parlé que vous ayez fini que vous ayez entendu
   qu'ils aient parlé   qu'ils aient fini   qu'ils aient entendu

PLUPERFECT

that I (might) *have spoken, etc.*	*that I (might)* *have finished, etc.*	*that I (might)* *have heard, etc.*
que j'eusse parlé	que j'eusse fini	que j'eusse entendu
que tu eusses parlé	que tu eusses fini	que tu eusses entendu
qu'il eût parlé	qu'il eût fini	qu'il eût entendu
nous eussions parlé[1]	nous eussions fini[1]	nous eussions entendu[1]
vous eussiez parlé	vous eussiez fini	vous eussiez entendu
ils eussent parlé	ils eussent fini	ils eussent entendu

IMPERATIVE

parle, *speak*   finis, *finish*   entends, *hear*
parlons, *let us speak* finissons, *let us finish* entendons, *let us hear*
parlez, *speak*   finissez, *finish*   entendez, *hear*

34. The Passive Voice

INFINITIVES

PRESENT   PAST

être aimé(e)(s), *to be loved* avoir été aimé(e)(s), *to have been loved*

PARTICIPLES

PRESENT   • PAST

étant aimé(e)(s), *being loved* ayant été aimé(e)(s), *having been loved*

INDICATIVE MOOD

PRESENT   PAST INDEFINITE

I am (being) loved, etc.   *I have been (was) loved, etc.*
   je suis aimé(e)   j'ai été aimé(e)

[1] **que** has been omitted to save space, but it should be used in conjugating these forms.

tu es aimé(e)
il (elle) est aimé(e)

nous sommes aimé(e)s
vous êtes aimé(e)s
ils (elles) sont aimé(e)s

tu as été aimé(e)
il (elle) a été aimé(e)

nous avons été aimé(e)s
vous avez été aimé(e)s
ils (elles) ont été aimé(e)s

IMPERFECT

I was (being) loved, etc.
j'étais aimé(e) etc.

PLUPERFECT

I had been loved, etc.
j'avais été aimé(e) etc.

PAST DEFINITE

I was loved, etc.
je fus aimé(e) etc.

PAST ANTERIOR

I had been loved, etc.
j'eus été aimé(e) etc.

FUTURE

I shall be loved, etc.
je serai aimé(e) etc.

FUTURE PERFECT

I shall have been loved, etc.
j'aurai été aimé(e) etc.

CONDITIONAL

I should be loved, etc.
je serais aimé(e), etc.

CONDITIONAL PERFECT

I should have been loved, etc.
j'aurais été aimé(e), etc.

SUBJUNCTIVE MOOD

PRESENT

that I (may) be loved, etc.
que je sois aimé(e), etc.

PERFECT

that I (may) have been loved, etc.
que j'aie été aimé(e), etc.

IMPERFECT

that I (might) be loved, etc.
que je fusse aimé(e), etc.

PLUPERFECT

that I (might) have been loved, etc.
que j'eusse été aimé(e), etc.

IMPERATIVE

sois aimé(e), *be loved*
soyons aimé(e)s, *let us be loved*
soyez aimé(e)s, *be loved*

35. The Reflexive Verb

INFINITIVES

PRESENT

PAST

se laver, *to wash oneself*   s'être lavé(e)(s), *to have washed oneself*

PARTICIPLES

PRESENT

PAST

se lavant, *washing oneself*   s'étant lavé(e)(s), *having washed oneself*

INDICATIVE MOOD

PRESENT

I wash (am washing) myself, etc.
je me lave
tu te laves
il se lave

nous nous lavons
vous vous lavez
ils se lavent

PAST INDEFINITE

I washed (have washed) myself, etc.
je me suis lavé(e)
tu t'es lavé(e)
il (elle) s'est lavé(e)

nous nous sommes lavé(e)s
vous vous êtes lavé(e)s
ils (elles) se sont lavé(e)s

IMPERFECT

I was washing (washed) myself, etc.
je me lavais, etc.

PLUPERFECT

I had washed myself etc.
je m'étais lavé(e), etc.

PAST DEFINITE

I washed myself, etc.
je me lavai, etc.

PAST ANTERIOR

I had washed myself, etc.
je me fus lavé(e), etc.

FUTURE

I shall wash myself, etc.
je me laverai, etc.

FUTURE PERFECT

I shall have washed myself, etc.
je me serai lavé(e), etc.

CONDITIONAL	CONDITIONAL PERFECT
I should wash myself, etc.	*I should have washed myself, etc.*
je me laverais, etc.	je me serais lavé(e), etc.

SUBJUNCTIVE MOOD

PRESENT	PAST
that I (may) wash myself, etc.	*that I (may) have washed myself, etc.*
que je me lave, etc.	que je me sois lavé(e), etc.

IMPERFECT	PLUPERFECT
that I (might) wash myself, etc.	*that I (might) have washed myself, etc.*
que je me lavasse, etc.	que je me fusse lavé(e), etc.

IMPERATIVE

lave-toi, *wash thyself (yourself)*
lavons-nous, *let us wash ourselves*
lavez-vous, *wash yourselves (yourself)*

36. Verbs in –ier, –ouer, and –uer

The vowels **i, ou, u** lose their full vowel value before a pronounced vowel and become semi-vowels, but they retain the full vowel value before a mute **e**.

copier, *to copy*	**jouer,** *to play*	**continuer,** *to continue*

PRESENT

je copie [kɔpi]	joue [ʒu]	continue [kɔ̃tiny]
tu copies [kɔpi]	joues [ʒu]	continues [kɔ̃tiny]
il copie [kɔpi]	joue [ʒu]	continue [kɔ̃tiny]
nous copions [kɔpjɔ̃]	jouons [ʒwɔ̃]	continuons [kɔ̃tinɥɔ̃]
vous copiez [kɔpje]	jouez [ʒwe]	continuez [kɔ̃tinɥe]
ils copient [kɔpi]	jouent [ʒu]	continuent [kɔ̃tiny]

IMPERFECT

je copiais [kɔpjɛ]	jouais [ʒwɛ]	continuais [kɔ̃tinɥɛ]
etc.	etc.	etc.

FUTURE

je copierai [kɔpire] etc.	jouerai [ʒure] etc.	continuerai [kɔ̃tinyre] etc.

CONDITIONAL

je copierais [kɔpirɛ] etc.	jouerais [ʒurɛ] etc.	continuerais [kɔ̃tinyrɛ] etc.

PAST PARTICIPLE

copié [kɔpje]	jou [ʒwe]	continué [kɔ̃tinɥe]

37. Orthographic (Spelling) Changes in Verbs

1. Verbs ending in **-cer,** *e.g.* **avancer** [avɑ̃se], *advance*, must preserve the [s] sound of **c** throughout their conjugation, and hence **c** becomes **ç** when it precedes **a** or **o** of an ending, but not elsewhere.

PRES. PART.	PRES. INDIC.	IMPF. INDIC.	PAST DEF.	IMPF. SUBJ.
avançant	avance	avançais	avançai	avançasse
	avances	avançais	avanças	avançasses
	avance	avançait	avança	avançât
	avançons	avancions	avançâmes	avançassions
	avancez	avanciez	avançâtes	avançassiez
	avancent	avançaient	avancèrent	avançassent

NOTE. Pronoun subjects are omitted to save space.

2. Verbs ending in **–ger,** *e.g.* **manger** [mɑ̃ʒe], *eat*, must preserve the [ʒ] sound of **g** throughout their conjugation, and hence **g** becomes **ge** when it precedes **a** or **o** of an ending, but not elsewhere.

PRES. PART.	PRES. INDIC.	IMPF. INDIC.	PAST DEF.	IMPF. SUBJ.
mangeant	mange	mangeais	mangeai	mangeasse
	manges	mangeais	mangeas	mangeasses
	mange	mangeait	mangea	mangeât

mangeons	mangions	mangeâmes	mangeassions
mangez	mangiez	mangeâtes	mangeassiez
mangent	mangeaient	mangèrent	mangeassent

3. Verbs ending in –oyer and –uyer, *e.g.* **nettoyer,** *clean,* **essuyer,** *wipe,* change **y** to **i** whenever it comes before **e** mute in conjugation, but not elsewhere; verbs in –ayer, *e.g.* **payer,** *pay,* may retain **y** throughout, or change **y** to **i** before **e** mute.

PRES. INDIC.	PRES. SUBJ.	FUTURE	CONDITIONAL
nettoie	nettoie	nettoierai	nettoierais
nettoies	nettoies	nettoieras	nettoierais
nettoie	nettoie	nettoiera	nettoierait
nettoyons	nettoyions	nettoierons	nettoierions
nettoyez	nettoyiez	nettoierez	nettoieriez
nettoient	nettoient	nettoieront	nettoieraient
essuie	essuie	essuierai	essuierais
etc.	etc.	etc.	etc.
paie / paye } etc.	paie / paye } etc.	paierai / payerai } etc.	paierais / payerais } etc.

4. Verbs having the stem vowel **e,** *e.g.* **mener,** *lead,* change this **e** to **è** wherever in conjugating the verb it is followed by a syllable containing **e** mute (but for verbs in –eler, –eter, see below).

PRES. INDIC.	PRES. SUBJ.	FUTURE	CONDITIONAL
mène	mène	mènerai	mènerais
mènes	mènes	mèneras	mènerais
mène	mène	mènera	mènerait
menons	menions	mènerons	mènerions
menez	meniez	mènerez	mèneriez
mènent	mènent	mèneront	mèneraient

5. Verbs having the stem vowel **é** followed by a consonant, *e.g.* **céder,** *yield,* change **é** to **è** in the present indicative and subjunctive, but retain **é** in the future and conditional when followed by a syllable containing **e** mute.

PRES. INDIC.	PRES. SUBJ.	FUTURE	CONDITIONAL
cède, etc.	cède, etc.	céderai, etc.	céderais, etc.

Note. Verbs with stem vowel é + vowel are regular *e.g.* **créer.**

6. Verbs in **–eler, –eter,** *e.g.* **appeler,** *call,* **jeter,** *throw,* usually double **l** or **t** before an **e** mute syllable in conjugation (but for some important exceptions, see below).

PRES. INDIC.	PRES. SUBJ.	FUTURE	CONDITIONAL
appelle	appelle	appellerai	appellerais
appelles	appelles	appelleras	appellerais
appelle	appelle	appellera	appellerait
appelons	appelions	appellerons	appellerions
appelez	appeliez	appellerez	appelleriez
appellent	appellent	appelleront	appelleraient

So also **jeter:**

jette, etc.	jette, etc.	jetterai, etc.	jetterais, etc.

7. A few verbs in **–eler, –eter** (the commonest being **geler,** *freeze,* **acheter,** *buy*) take the grave accent like **mener.**

PRES. INDIC.	PRES. SUBJ.	FUTURE	CONDITIONAL
gèle, etc.	gèle, etc.	gèlerai, etc.	gèlerais, etc.
achète etc.	achète, etc.	achèterai, etc.	achèterais, etc.

—PRINCIPAL IRREGULAR VERBS—

INFINITIVE	PARTICIPLES	PRESENT INDICATIVE	
acquérir, *to acquire*	**acquérant** **acquis, –e**	**j'acquiers** tu acquiers il acquiert	nous acquérons vous acquérez ils acquièrent
aller, *to go*	**allant** **allé, –e**	**je vais** tu vas il va	nous allons vous allez ils vont
s'asseoir, *to sit down*	**s'asseyant**[1] **assis, –e**	**je m'assieds** tu t'assieds il s'assied	nous nous asseyons vous vous asseyez ils s'asseyent[2]
avoir, *to have*	**ayant** **eu, –e**	**j'ai** tu as il a	nous avons vous avez ils ont
battre, *to beat*	**battant** **battu, –e**	**je bats** tu bats il bat	nous battons vous battez ils battent
boire, *to drink*	**buvant** **bu, –e**	**je bois** tu bois il boit	nous buvons vous buvez ils boivent
conduire, *to conduct*	**conduisant** **conduit, –e**	**je conduis** tu conduis il conduit	nous conduisons vous conduisez ils conduisent
connaître, *to know*	**connaissant** **connu, –e**	**je connais** tu connais il connaît	nous connaissons vous connaissez ils connaissent

[1] *Or* s'assoyant.   [2] *Or* je m'assois, tu t'assois, il s'assoit, nous nous assoyons, vous vous assoyez, ils s'assoient.

Past Definite	Future	Present Subjunctive	Imperative
j'acquis	j'acquerrai	que j'acquière que nous acquérions qu'ils acquièrent	acquiers acquérons acquérez
j'allai	j'irai	que j'aille que nous allions qu'ils aillent	va allons allez
je m'assis	je m'assiérai (asseyerai) (assoirai)	que je m'asseye nous nous asseyions[3] qu'ils s'asseyent[4]	assieds-toi asseyons-nous asseyez-vous[5]
j'eus	j'aurai	que j'aie que nous ayons qu'ils aient	aie ayons ayez
je battis	je battrai	que je batte que nous battions qu'ils battent	bats battons battez
je bus	je boirai	que je boive que nous buvions qu'ils boivent	bois buvons buvez
je conduisis	je conduirai	que je conduise que nous conduisions qu'ils conduisent	conduis conduisons conduisez
je connus	je connaîtrai	que je connaisse que nous connaissions qu'ils connaissent	connais connaissons connaissez

[3] **que** omitted for space.   [4] *Or* que je m'assoie, que nous nous assoyions, qu'ils s'assoient.   [5] *Or* assois-toi, assoyons-nous, assoyez-vous.

INFINITIVE	PARTICIPLES	PRESENT INDICATIVE	

construire, *to construct*, is conjugated like **conduire**

coudre, *to sew*	**cousant** **cousu,** –e	**je couds** tu couds il coud	nous cousons vous cousez ils cousent
courir, *to run*	**courant** **couru**	**je cours** tu cours il court	nous courons vous courez ils courent
couvrir, *to cover*	**couvrant** **couvert,** –e	**je couvre** tu couvres il couvre	nous couvrons vous couvrez ils couvrent
craindre, *to fear*	**craignant** **craint,** –e	**je crains** tu crains il craint	nous craignons vous craignez ils craignent
croire, *to believe*	**croyant** **cru,** –e	**je crois** tu crois il croit	nous croyons vous croyez ils croient
devoir, *to owe must*	**devant** **dû,** due	**je dois** tu dois il doit	nous devons vous devez ils doivent
dire, *to say*	**disant** **dit,** –e	**je dis** tu dis il dit	nous disons vous dites ils disent
dormir, *to sleep*	**dormant** **dormi**	**je dors** tu dors il dort	nous dormons vous dormez ils dorment

PAST DEFINITE	FUTURE	PRESENT SUBJUNCTIVE	IMPERATIVE
je cousis	je coudrai	que je couse	couds cousons cousez
je courus	je courrai	que je coure que nous courions qu'ils courent	cours courons courez
je couvris	je couvrirai	que je couvre que nous couvrions qu'ils couvrent	couvre couvrons couvrez
je craignis	je craindrai	que je craigne que nous craignions qu'ils craignent	crains craignons craignez
je crus	je croirai	que je croie que nous croyions qu'ils croient	crois croyons croyez
je dus	je devrai	que je doive que nous devions qu'ils doivent	dois devons devez
je dis	je dirai	que je dise que nous disions qu'ils disent	dis disons dites
je dormis	je dormirai	que je dorme que nous dormions qu'ils dorment	dors dormons dormez

Infinitive	Participles	Present Indicative	
écrire, *to write*	**écrivant** **écrit,** –e	**j'écris** tu écris il écrit	nous écrivons vous écrivez ils écrivent
envoyer, *to send*	**envoyant** **envoyé,** –e	**j'envoie** tu envoies il envoie	nous envoyons vous envoyez ils envoient
être, *to be*	**étant** **été**	**je suis** tu es il est	nous sommes vous êtes ils sont
faire, *to do*	**faisant** **fait,** –e	**je fais** tu fais il fait	nous faisons vous faites ils font
falloir, *to be necessary*	—— **fallu**	**il faut**	
lire, *to read*	**lisant** **lu,** –e	**je lis** tu lis il lit	nous lisons vous lisez ils lisent
mettre, *to put*	**mettant** **mis,** –e	**je mets** tu mets il met	nous mettons vous mettez ils mettent
mourir, *to die*	**mourant** **mort,** –e	**je meurs** tu meurs il meurt	nous mourons vous mourez ils meurent

offrir, *to offer,* conjugated like **couvrir**

ouvrir, *to open,* conjugated like **couvrir**

paraître, *to appear,* conjugated like **connaître**

Past Definite	Future	Present Subjunctive	Imperative
j'écrivis	j'écrirai	que j'écrive que nous écrivions qu'ils écrivent	écris écrivons écrivez
j'envoyai	j'enverrai	que j'envoie que nous envoyions qu'ils envoient	envoie envoyons envoyez
je fus	je serai (*Impf.*) j'étais	que je sois que nous soyons qu'ils soient	sois soyons soyez
je fis	je ferai	que je fasse que nous fassions qu'ils fassent	fais faisons faites
il fallut	il faudra	qu'il faille	
je lus	je lirai	que je lise que nous lisions qu'ils lisent	lis lisons lisez
je mis	je mettrai	que je mette que nous mettions qu'ils mettent	mets mettons mettez
je mourus	je mourrai	que je meure que nous mourions qu'ils meurent	meurs mourons mourez

INFINITIVE	PARTICIPLES	PRESENT INDICATIVE	
partir, *to set out*	**partant** **parti,** –e	conjugated like **dormir**	
plaire, *to please*	**plaisant** **plu**	**je plais** tu plais il plaît	nous plaisons vous plaisez ils plaisent
pleuvoir, *to rain*	**pleuvant** **plu**	**il pleut**	
pouvoir, *to be able*	**pouvant** **pu**	**je peux (puis)** tu peux il peut	nous pouvons vous pouvez ils peuvent
prendre, *to take*	**prenant** **pris,** –e	**je prends** tu prends il prend	nous prenons vous prenez ils prennent
recevoir, *to receive*	**recevant** **reçu,** –e	**je reçois** tu reçois il reçoit	nous recevons vous recevez ils reçoivent
rire, *to laugh*	**riant** **ri**	**je ris** tu ris il rit	nous rions vous riez ils rient
savoir, *to know*	**sachant** **su,** –e	**je sais** tu sais il sait	nous savons vous savez ils savent
sentir, *to feel*	**sentant** **senti,** –e	**je sens** conjugated like **dormir**	
servir, *to serve*	**servant** **servi,** –e	**je sers** conjugated like **dormir**	

Past Definite	Future	Present Subjunctive	Imperative
je plus	je plairai	que je plaise	plais plaisons plaisez
il plut	il plcuvra	qu'il pleuve	
je pus	je pourrai	que je puisse que nous puissions qu'ils puissent	——
je pris	je prendrai	que je prenne que nous prenions qu'ils prennent	prends prenons prenez
je reçus	je recevrai	que je reçoive que nous recevions qu'ils reçoivent	reçois recevons recevez
je ris	je rirai	que je rie que nous riions qu'ils rient	ris rions riez
je sus	je saurai	que je sache que nous sachions qu'ils sachent	sache sachons sachez
je sentis			
je servis			

INFINITIVE	PARTICIPLES	PRESENT INDICATIVE	
sortir, *to go out*	**sortant** **sorti,** –e	**je sors** conjugated like **dormir**	
souffrir, *to suffer*	**souffrant** **souffert,** –e	**je souffre** conjugated like **couvrir**	
suivre, *to follow*	**suivant** **suivi,**-e	**je suis** tu suis il suit	nous suivons vous suivez ils suivent
tenir, *to hold*	**tenant** **tenu,** –e	**je tiens** tu tiens il tient	nous tenons vous tenez ils tiennent
venir, *to come*	**venant** **venu,** –e	**je viens** conjugated like **tenir**	
voir, *to see*	**voyant** **vu,** –e	**je vois** tu vois il voit	nous voyons vous voyez ils voient
vouloir, *to be willing*	**voulant** **voulu,** –e	**je veux** tu veux il veut	nous voulons vous voulez ils veulent

Past Definite	Future	Present Subjunctive	Imperative
je sortis			
je souffris			
je suivis	je suivrai	que je suive que nous suivions qu'ils suivent	suis suivons suivez
je tins nous tînmes ils tinrent	je tiendrai	que je tienne que nous tenions qu'ils tiennent	tiens tenons tenez
je vins			
je vis	je verrai	que je voie que nous voyions qu'ils voient	vois voyons voyez
je voulus	je voudrai	que je veuille que nous voulions qu'ils veuillent	veuille veuillons veuillez

FORMULES DE CORRESPONDANCE

FORMS OF LETTERS

I. En s'adressant à un homme:
  A. *En-tête.* — L'en-tête varie selon le degré des relations sociales entre correspondants.

  1. Monsieur; Cher Monsieur; Cher Monsieur et ami; Cher ami. On ne dit jamais: Mon cher Monsieur. Il faut aussi éviter de dire: Cher Monsieur Dupont, etc.
  2. Monsieur; Mon cher Docteur (Maître pour avocats); Cher Docteur (Maître) et ami; Mon cher Confrère (entre docteurs et avocats).
  3. Monsieur le Président (le Ministre le Sénateur le Directeur, etc.)

  B. *Formules finales.* — On répète toujours, dans la formule finale, les mêmes mots qui ont servi pour l'en-tête.
  Voici les formules les plus habituelles dans l'ordre du degré des relations sociales entre correspondants.

  1. Je vous prie d'agréer, Monsieur, l'expression de mes sentiments respectueux.

2. Recevez, Monsieur, l'assurance de ma considération la plus distinguée (de mes sentiments les plus distingués).
3. Recevez, cher Monsieur, l'assurance de mes meilleurs sentiments (de mes sentiments très cordiaux).
4. Recevez, cher ami, l'assurance de ma plus cordiale sympathie.
5. Dans une lettre intime et familière on peut terminer à l'américaine: Cordialement vôtre; Bien sincèrement à vous, etc.

II. En s'adressant à une femme:
A. *En-tête.*

Madame; Chère Madame; Chère Madame et amie; Chère amie.
On ne dit jamais: Chère Madame Dupont, etc.

B. *Formules finales.*

1. Je vous prie d'agréer, . . ., mes hommages les plus respectueux.
2. Je vous prie d'agréer, . . ., avec mes hommages l'expression de ma plus respectueuse sympathie.
    A un degré plus intime, le cœur dictera la formule.

Correspondance commerciale

A. *Commande de marchandises.*

Lyon, le 10 janvier 19—
Messieurs Lenoir, Leblanc et Cie

Messieurs,

Je vous prie de m'expédier le plus tôt possible par express les articles suivants: . . .
Comme j'ai un besoin pressant de ces marchandises ayez l'obligeance de me faire savoir par retour du courrier si je puis compter les recevoir avant la fin du mois.

S'il vous est impossible de les livrer avant le 28 courant vous voudrez bien considérer mon ordre comme nul et non avenu.

Veuillez agréer, Messieurs, l'expression de mes sentiments distingués.

B. *Réponse à la lettre précédente.*

Monsieur

Conformément à votre demande du 10 courant nous avons l'honneur de vous informer que votre ordre sera exécuté dans le plus bref délai. Selon vos désirs les marchandises faisant l'objet de votre commande seront expédiées à votre charge par service rapide Lyon-Paris.

Nous vous prions d'agréer Monsieur nos salutations empressées.

Une Invitation

Le Colonel et Madame de Beaupré prient Monsieur et Madame Richardson de leur faire l'honneur de venir dîner chez eux le samedi quinze mars prochain à huit heures et demie.

Réponse à l'invitation précédente

A. *Acceptation.*

Monsieur et Madame Paul V. Richardson présentent leurs meilleurs compliments au Colonel et à Madame de Beaupré et les remercient de leur aimable invitation à laquelle ils seront très heureux de se rendre.

B. *Refus.*

Monsieur et Madame Paul V. Richardson prient le Colonel et Madame de Beaupré d'agréer l'assurance de leur respectueuse sympathie et les remercient de leur invitation à laquelle its auront le regret de ne pouvoir se rendre, étant retenus par des engagements antérieurs.

Souhaits de fête

Permettez-moi de vous offrir à l'occasion de votre fête, mes meilleurs souhaits (mes vœux les plus sympathiques; mes souhaits les plus cordiaux; mes souhaits affectueux etc.).

Entre intimes, on pourra dire tout simplement: « Bonne et heureuse fête! »

I. Addressing a man:
   A. *Heading.* — The heading varies according to the degree of social relationship between correspondents.

   1. Sir; Dear Sir; Dear Sir and Friend; Dear Friend. One never says: My dear Sir. One must also avoid saying: Dear Mr. Dupont, etc.
   2. Sir; My dear Doctor (*Maître* for lawyers); Dear Doctor (*Maître*) and Friend; My dear Colleague (among doctors and lawyers).
   3. Mr. President (Minister, Senator, Director, etc.).

   B. *Endings.* — The same words that have been used in the heading are always repeated in the ending.

   The most usual forms in the order of the degree of social relationship between correspondents are these:

   1. Yours respectfully (lit. " I beg you to accept, Sir, the expression of my respectful sentiments ").
   2. Sincerely yours, Very truly yours (lit. " Receive, Sir, the assurance of . . .").
   3. Very sincerely yours (lit. " Receive, dear Sir, the assurance of . . .").
   4. Cordially yours (lit. " Receive, dear friend, the assurance . . .").
   5. In a familiar and intimate letter one can end in the American fashion: Cordially yours; Yours sincerely, etc.

II. Addressing a woman:
   A. *Heading.*

   Madam; Dear Madam; Dear Madam and Friend; Dear Friend.

   One never says: Dear Madam Dupont, etc.

B. *Endings.*

1. Yours respectfully (lit. " I beg you to accept, etc.").
2. Sincerely yours (lit. " I beg you to accept, etc.").

In a more intimate degree, the heart will dictate the form.

Commercial Correspondence

A. *An order for merchandise.*

Lyons, January 10, 19—
Lenoir, Leblanc & Co.

Gentlemen:

Please send me the following articles as soon as possible by express: . . .

As I am in urgent need of this merchandise will you please let me know by return mail whether I can count on receiving it before the end of the month.

If it is impossible for you to deliver it before the 28th of this month, will you please consider my order as cancelled.

Very truly yours,

B. *Reply to the preceding letter.*

Dear Sir,

Complying with your request of the 10th of this month we are glad (lit. " honored ") to inform you that your order will be filled as soon as possible. In accordance with your wishes the merchandise you ordered will be sent at your expense by the Lyons-Paris express.

Yours truly

An Invitation

Colonel and Mrs. de Beaupré request the honor of Mr. and Mrs. Richardson's company at dinner on next Saturday, March fifteenth, at half past eight o'clock.

Reply to the Preceding Invitation

A. *Accepting.*

Mr. and Mrs. Paul V. Richardson present their compliments to Colonel and Mrs. de Beaupré and thank them for their kind invitation, which they are happy to accept.

B. *Declining.*

Mr. and Mrs. Paul V. Richardson present their compliments to Colonel and Mrs. de Beaupré and thank them for their invitation, which they regret not being able to accept because of previous engagements.

Birthday (*or* Name-Day) Greetings

Many happy returns of the day, etc.

Among intimate friends one can simply say: " Happy birthday! "

on the way to Rouen. from Amiens

Aumale
Neufchaten - en - Bray
Prerreval

Towards Mont St. Michele

Pontorson or Beauvoir